NANCY KERRIGAN
GOLDEN GIRL

"When Kerrigan ⬚⬚⬚ regimen left her w⬚⬚⬚ ⬚⬚⬚ the malls. 'I lost a lot o⬚⬚⬚ ⬚⬚rted skating,' says Nancy. 'Bu⬚⬚ ⬚anted to skate. It was an irresistible cha⬚⬚nge.'"

—*People* magazine

"Blessed with long, slender limbs and a natural elegance, Nancy also reaps the rewards of a photogenic beauty that last year won her standing as one of *People* magazine's '50 Most Beautiful People in the World.'"

—*Time* magazine

"Since she was attacked, Nancy has kept it all together. When I speak to her on the phone she sounds great, she sounds up, like the Nancy we know, and that's what's so encouraging. This hasn't thrown her for a loop."

—Paul Wylie, Nancy's training
partner and an Olympic silver
medalist in men's figure skating
(*Newsweek* magazine)

Dreams of Gold

The NANCY KERRIGAN Story

WAYNE COFFEY & FILIP BONDY

ST. MARTIN'S PAPERBACKS

DREAMS OF GOLD: THE NANCY KERRIGAN STORY

Copyright © 1994 by Wayne Coffey and Filip Bondy.

Front cover photograph of Nancy Kerrigan copyright © 1992 Craig Blankenhorn/Black Star. Inset photograph of Tonya Harding by Brent Wojahn/*The Oregonian*/Sygma. Back cover photograph of Kerrigan by Dwayne Burleson/Sygma; back cover photograph of Harding by Steve Nehl/*The Oregonian*/Sygma.

ISBN: 0-312-95399-2

Printed in the United States of America

St. Martin's Paperbacks edition/March 1994

10 9 8 7 6 5 4 3 2

For Bianca Berger
F.B.

For Denise and Alexandra
W.C.

ACKNOWLEDGMENTS

A number of people contributed time, support and research assistance to this book; without them it would not have been possible. To Professors Charles Euchner and Amy Singleton of the College of Holy Cross; Jeff Gutridge, editor of the *Stoneham Independent*; Kevin Whitmer, sports editor of the *New York Daily News*—many thanks. Mark Starr of *Newsweek* has been a friend and resource in the figure-skating world long before this undertaking. Finally, thank you to our families, for the understanding and tolerance. It's okay to look now.

Contents

One

The Courage to Come Back

It was a frigid, cloudless Thursday in Stoneham, Massachusetts, a dead-of-winter day that left the whole town looking like a patch of suburban tundra. Streets and sidewalks were scarred with ice. Mounds of snow had long since hardened into roadside walls. Every now and then a car went by that wasn't blotched white with salt, and people would notice. Imagine that. A clean car.

At Dave's Place, an oldtime breakfast counter in the heart of downtown, people sat on stools and talked about fuel bills and deceased batteries and backs done in by too much shoveling. Just outside, people wondered when the temperature might get out of single digits, as if the speculating could possibly help.

But three weeks into 1994, in a January that had become chilling for reasons far beyond the climate, the people in Stoneham were focusing primarily on Nancy Kerrigan. Her picture was on what seemed like every other wall and window in town. Inside the picture was a heart, on a poster with the words "We Love You, Nancy" on top. Folks who wouldn't know a double axel from a double play were eagerly following news accounts of her progress: How's the knee? How's the therapy? What's it looking like for the Olympics? *Do you really think she's going to be able to make it back?*

Stoneham is a solid, salt-of-the-earth town, quaint without being phony. It has been around since 1725, which no doubt contributes to the unmistakable sense of history, of community. It's there in Hank's Bakery, serving up delectables for close to seventy-five years now, and at the *Stoneham Independent,* "your hometown newspaper since 1870." Stoneham used to be a big shoe-manufacturing town, but after those companies left, smaller operations became the lifeblood of the community. And it survived. Over the half-dozen Main Street blocks, even on the strip malls out of town, there is a rugged reliability about the place. As one young resident, a college student, said,

"It sounds corny, but this is a town where everybody knows each other and just about everybody cares about each other. It's always been that way."

Nancy Kerrigan has spent her whole life in Stoneham. The news about her on Thursday, January 20, could hardly have been better. Back on the ice at Stoneham Arena, where everything had started for her, Nancy had done a two-and-one-half-revolution double axel. She had performed some of her most difficult jumps, and she had repeatedly landed on her right leg, with no problems. Who could've imagined that? Days earlier, the forecast was that she wouldn't be getting near such demanding moves for another week or so. Days before that, people weren't even sure she would have any shot at competing in the Olympics. And here she was, back in her white skating outfit, spinning and springing, sharing the satisfaction with her longtime coaches, Evy and Mary Scotvold. "I did a little bit more today," Nancy told reporters. "I feel great."

"It's very encouraging," said Vincent Buscemi, her physical therapist.

"Her hardest jump is the double axel, and she landed that today and did it beautifully," said her father, Dan Kerrigan. "Her knee is a little stiff, but she's doing great."

In truth, the interest in Nancy's progress

went far beyond the sturdy boundaries of Stoneham, fifteen miles north of Boston. Nancy Kerrigan was no longer merely Stoneham's brown-haired girl next door, from the pea-green clapboard house on Cedar Avenue, the kid whom half the neighborhood had driven to skating practice at one point or another. As much as some folks might have wanted to throw a protective cloak around her, keep her as their own, it couldn't be that way, not anymore. She had moved into an entirely different realm. She was receiving get-well notes from Ronald and Nancy Reagan, who wrote, "We're so thankful you weren't harmed. We both know how difficult it can be to live in the public eye." She was hearing from plenty of other big deals, past and present. The "we're behind you" phone calls were nonstop. Flowers, candy, cookies—stuff was flooding in from admirers she didn't even know she had, from places she had never heard of. And more than that was flooding in: Nancy's agent, Jerry Solomon of ProServ, reported that in one fax-crazy weekend, he had received nearly three dozen offers for film rights to her life story. Film crews and photographers and reporters were camped out on Cedar Avenue, behind a barrier the Stoneham police had put up so the Kerrigans might have a modicum of privacy. She had become as much of an evening news fixture as President Clinton. Suddenly, everything about Nancy Kerrigan was big news.

It was all so strange, so surreal, this unforeseen vault into megastardom. But hadn't everything been surreal since the afternoon of January 6, when twenty-four-year-old Nancy Kerrigan was bashed in the knee by a thug wielding a blunt stick—when what may go down as the most heinous and bizarre crime ever perpetrated against an American athlete began to unfold?

A blizzard was raging outside Cobo Arena in Detroit that afternoon as Nancy Kerrigan came off the ice following a practice session in preparation for the U.S. Figure Skating Association Championships. In two days, the top two women at the competition would be named to the U.S. Olympic team. The defending national champion and a bronze medalist at the 1992 Winter Olympics in Albertville, France, Nancy was coming in with what all agreed was greater determination and better conditioning than ever before. Her last major competition, the 1993 World Championships, had been an unmitigated disaster. She had made a few early mistakes, and then her entire routine had fallen apart as her nerves unraveled. She'd wound up finishing fifth, a performance so disappointing to her that the rinkside audio feed had picked up her voice sobbing, "I just want to die!"

That was the memory Nancy wanted to put to permanent rest at the U.S. National Championships in Detroit. Instead, she came away with an immeasurably worse memory—of a muscle-bound man and a black club, of the horrific sound of her own voice crying, "Why me? Why now?" Moments later, as Dan Kerrigan bent over to pick up his daughter in his meaty, workingman arms, she said to him, "It hurts so bad. I'm so scared." She asked why a few more times. She was all but inconsolable. It was an entirely understandable feeling.

Said Brenda Kerrigan, Nancy's mother, "We can't believe that any human being would de-liberately—*deliberately*—hurt her."

In the ensuing weeks, of course, a portrait of the crime emerged that would be laughable if it weren't so sad. Authorities have arrested four people, including Jeff Gillooly and Shawn Eckardt, the former husband and bodyguard, respectively, of Nancy Kerrigan's principal American rival, Tonya Harding. The alleged mission was to maim Harding's foremost obstacle to winning the nationals. Though no firm evidence had surfaced linking Harding to the crime as this book went to press, Eckardt reportedly told authorities that Harding not only knew of the conspiracy, but was getting impatient that it was taking so long to carry out. Harding did little to improve her image when she waited three full weeks after the attack to convey even a trace of compassion for Nancy Kerrigan.

However things turn out in the legal arena, the Kerrigan story has forever sullied the glittering, glamorous world of figure skating. Recently a major maker of champagne signed on as a principal sponsor of the USFSA. What's next, Jiffy Lube?

The lone positive to come of the episode is a sincere and deeply felt national appreciation for Nancy Kerrigan. Millions of people across the country have come to admire her strength and resilience, the way she has refused to give in. At a jam-packed press conference just over twenty-four hours after the attack, Nancy answered questions bravely, no matter how much they dragged her back into the nightmare. Wearing a stylish patchwork jacket, her tousled brown hair falling just below her shoulders, she spoke with a demure kind of defiance. At five feet four inches tall and a sleek 111 pounds, Kerrigan looked stunning, which was nothing new. The warrior-type resolve, *that* was new.

"I'll do anything I can to get myself mentally and physically ready," she said. Not long after, Evy Scotvold echoed the sentiment.

"We can't let a vicious criminal assault decide they can take someone off the Olympic team," he said. "If she heals, she can go. She has to go. Otherwise, she'd be honoring the attack."

Even the throng of reporters—a skeptical lot, to say the least—came away impressed by Kerrigan's fortitude and good humor throughout a traumatic time. Who didn't smile when Nancy was talking to Connie Chung on the CBS program "Eye to Eye" a few weeks before the Olympics? Asked about her well-being, Nancy replied, "I'm in very good shape, because he had such bad aim."

To be sure, Nancy already had plenty of fans, long before Shawn Eckardt started showing up on the nation's television screens. She is, after all, a champion, an Olympian, a woman with an almost regal gracefulness on ice and looks so striking that she has often been compared to the young Katharine Hepburn. Last year, Nancy was named one of *People* magazine's "50 Most Beautiful People." She has endorsement deals ranging from Reebok to Seiko to Campbell's soup. She has a pleasant, unassuming personality; comes from a loving, hardworking family. Though the Kerrigans' collective story was well chronicled at the Olympics two years ago, nothing has changed to diminish its poignancy. There is Dan Kerrigan, a welder by trade, who worked two and sometimes three jobs, took out loans, and did whatever was necessary to cover Nancy's training expenses. There is Brenda Kerrigan, Nancy's mother, who is legally blind and must press her face against the television screen to make out her daughter's movements. The whole family, including older brothers Mark and Michael, has never wavered in its support of Nancy's dream to compete, and win, in the Olympics.

≈

There is something about female figure skaters that commands a unique hold on the American public. From the late 1940s through the early 1990s, figure skaters have without question been the most popular of all women athletes. Tenley Albright, Carol Heiss, Peggy Fleming, Dorothy Hamill, Kristi Yamaguchi—each has parlayed Olympic stardom into celebrity well beyond the ice. The expression *skating sweetheart* no doubt has a patronizing ring to some, but it captures the essence of the ubiquitous appeal these women have generated. All of them were undeniably dedicated athletes who exhibited dazzling skill and grace. Each also had her own eye-catching beauty that made her fascinating to watch. Peggy Fleming seemed statuesque, almost ethereal. Dorothy Hamill was perky and buoyant, hopelessly cute. This is not to reduce the sport to cheese-cake on ice: it is simply the way it is.

Figure skating has long been a strange hybrid: many parts high athletic drama, a few parts fashion show and sex appeal. Somewhere in the mix is vulnerability, too, which only adds to the allure. Figure skaters are out there all alone; their sport is an unforgiving one. A basketball player can miss a dunk or a football player can drop a pass, and in all but the rarest of instances, the humiliation and/or horror is short-lived and usually semiprivate. Even when Gail Devers lost a chance for a second Olympic gold medal when she hit the last hurdle and went sprawling on the Barcelona track in the summer of 1992, at least there were other hurdlers around to deflect some of the attention. When a figure skater fouls up, there is no place to hide. She's on her rear end, and the whole world knows it. The vulnerability extends even to the so-called kiss and cry area, where skaters await their marks from the sport's notoriously unpredictable judges and, depending on the results, break into kisses and squeals or heaves and sobs.

Enthusiasts may argue over which factor contributes most to figure skating's popularity, but there's no disputing that Nancy Kerrigan is heiress to the skating throne held previously by Fleming, Yamaguchi, and the rest.

Like every other competitor, Nancy heads into Hamar Ice Rink in Lillehammer, Norway, knowing that the sport's emotional poles are never greater than at the Olympic Games. The ladies' Olympic competition begins with the original program, seven P.M. local time on Wednesday, February 23. It concludes with the freestyle program at the same time, two days later. How will Nancy Kerrigan do? How much will the lost training time hurt her? How will she be able to deal with what promises to be perhaps the harshest media glare that any Olympic athlete has ever known? It got old having camera crews camped at the foot of the family driveway in Stoneham. What will it be like being tailed by camera crews from around the globe? What will it feel like knowing that half the world will be tuning in to see how she holds up? In a normal Olympic year, figure skating receives higher ratings than any other sporting event on American television outside of the Super Bowl. This year—far from normal—even the mighty NFL may be overshadowed.

So the questions continue. Will there be any more of the recurring nightmares Nancy has had since the attack? Will she be able to purge her mind of the slimeballs who did this to her? Elaine Zayak, a longtime friend of Kerrigan's who placed sixth in the 1984 Olympic Games in Sarajevo, thinks it is almost impossible. "*I* wouldn't be able to do it," she said. "I'd be watching my back the whole time."

We have grown accustomed to hearing the modern athlete talk about focus and tunnel vision. Nancy Kerrigan won't need tunnel vision to escape the sideshow that will surround her in Lillehammer. She will need core-of-the-earth vision. She will need to keep her Olympic existence as simple and uncluttered as possible. It wouldn't hurt to heed the words of her Bay State ancestor Henry David Thoreau, who wrote in *Walden*, "It is life near the bone where it is sweetest."

Said Nancy, "When I'm on the ice, nothing really affects me. I just have to concentrate on skating. I just kept skating so many years because I loved it." That is pretty near the bone.

Amid the intense interest surrounding Nancy Kerrigan as these games begin, beyond the overwhelming curiosity, shines one unwavering beacon of truth: millions upon millions of people will be rooting for her. They'll pull for her to win a gold medal, of course, but many of her fans will simply be hoping that she will enjoy herself and do her best, and let the medal stand take care of itself. Some of the partisans will be figure-skating fans who go back to Albright and Heiss. Others, like Lizaida Valentin, will be watching figure skating for the first time. Lizaida is nine years old, a fourth-grader at the Enrico Fermi School in Yonkers, New York, just north of New York City. She has never watched the Olympics before. She had never heard of Nancy Kerrigan before January 6 but has learned a lot about her since. "When I saw what happened, it was like 'Oh my God, what a terrible thing to happen,'" said Lizaida. "I'll be rooting for her because I think it will be nice for her to come back and be in the Olympics."

Two

A New Ice Age
in Stoneham

The Monday morning after the assault, Nancy put on black tights, black gloves, and a green-and-blue warm-up jacket, walked through a low white door, and stepped onto a fresh sheet of ice at Stoneham Arena. In big block letters on a wall behind her were the words "The Home of '92 Olympian, Nancy Kerrigan." A side street leading up to the arena was marked "Nancy Kerrigan Way." In a display case inside the front doors was a plaque saluting her bronze medal performance in Albertville. Working under the tutelage of the Scotvolds, Nancy had shifted her training to a rink on Cape Cod. But being back in Stoneham Arena was like putting on an old pair of slippers. This was where her father used to drive her for lessons at five-thirty in the morning, where she first conjured images of one day competing in the Olympics. It felt familiar. It felt right.

Nancy Kerrigan was six years old when she began figure-skating. One of her first instructors was Queenie Antonucci, whom everybody in Stoneham knows as Ducky. Ducky Antonucci has taught thousands of kids how to figure-skate across twenty-seven years. All these lessons later, Nancy still stands apart.

"I could see she had extraordinary talent," Antonucci told the *New York Daily News*. "She really took to the ice. Right from the start she could go out and do a twirl and a little jump. Even when she was fooling around you could see it. She learned to do triple toe loops when she was twelve or thirteen, and she could just pop them off as if they were nothing."

Theresa Martin, who founded the Stoneham Figure Skating Club, worked with Nancy individually for close to ten years. With the exception of the Scotvolds, Martin, now a bank vice president, was more responsible for Nancy's development than anyone else. "I remember the first day she came into a group lesson," Martin said. "She was wearing this little blue Danskin dress. She didn't want any part of it.

She was crying. She wanted to go back to her mom [who was standing by the edge of the rink]." Martin went over to the little girl and spoke a few reassuring words. The tears gradually stopped. Nancy participated in the class, though still somewhat reluctantly. "She told me once in the beginning, 'I want to play hockey. I don't want to figure-skate,'" Martin said with a chuckle. "I tried to explain to her that figure skating was more appropriate."

Both of Nancy's brothers, Mark and Michael, were athletic youngsters who loved playing hockey. Nancy wanted to be like them, so she would go around talking about hockey, too. Somehow that passing early interest has grown with every written retelling. It's gotten to the point that some accounts almost leave one thinking that Nancy's dream was to play in the National Hockey League. It's true that after the attack she received flowers from Adam Oates of the Boston Bruins, and also heard from Mark Messier of the New York Rangers, but that's about as close to hockey as she has come. "Her interest in hockey has been way overblown," Martin said.

It is equally curious to Martin the way that Kerrigan has been typecast as a sort of ballerina on ice, a glamour girl whose splendid looks help mask rather ordinary athletic ability. Just because Kerrigan has never landed a triple axel (three-and-a-half revolutions)—a move that only Tonya Harding and Midori Ito of Japan have ever performed in competition—doesn't mean that Kerrigan has any athletic deficiences. In fact, both Martin and Antonucci talk of a strong, gifted athlete who was doing jumps and combinations far ahead of many of her skating peers.

Kerrigan had skinny legs with long, sinewy muscles—"colt legs," Martin called them—and enjoyed using them for acrobatics of all varieties. She'd do cartwheels and walkovers before practice. She loved skiing and was very good at it. She never participated in team sports, because there was no way her skating schedule would let her.

Even at an early age, it was nothing for Kerrigan to practice for three or four hours a day. Later on, the norm was four to six hours, seven days a week. As dedicated as she was, what really served her well was that she never took herself too seriously. She gave it her best and left it at that, rarely plunging herself into fits of self-doubt and self-criticism. Of course she'd sometimes get upset if she was having difficulty with a particular aspect of her skating, but more often than not she was able to laugh about it. "Even now the image I picture of Nancy is her laughing, being silly," Martin told the *New York Daily News.*

Nancy was ten years old when she entered her first significant competition, the Boston Open. She skated beautifully and placed second. Not only did the pressure not faze her, it seemed to bring out the best in her. "She was always competitive," Ducky Antonucci said. "It seemed like every time out she came home with a gold, silver, or bronze." Looking back, a silver medal performance in the eastern championships may have been among the best of her early career. Sixteen-year-old Nancy was competing in the novice ladies division, and after the compulsory figures segment of the competition (mandatory routines, since eliminated, that required skaters to execute figure eights and other basic steps), she seemed hopelessly behind. With nothing to lose, she went out and performed a triple jump–triple jump combination in her long program, so impressing the judges that she vaulted all the way to second. Theresa Martin may have been most impressed of all: Nancy had never before attempted that combination—even in practice.

Nancy was not a skater who catapulted onto the national scene, as, for example, did thirteen-year-old Michelle Kwan in the summer of 1993 in San Antonio. The youngest competitor at the Olympic Festival, the four-foot-nine-inch, seventy-seven-pound Kwan jumped and spun her way into the hearts of twenty-five thousand people in the Alamadome, believed to be the largest figure-skating crowd in history. She instantly became the talk of the skating world, all the more so when it was learned how she'd come to be competing as a senior. Earlier in the year, when her venerable coach, Frank Carroll, went out of town, Michelle sneaked off and took the test required for a junior skater to move into the senior ranks. She did so very much against Carroll's wishes. Michelle passed the test and managed to survive the wrath of Carroll. Her festival showing proved she knew exactly what she was doing, as did her performance in the U.S. National Championships of January 1994; her second-place finish was a stunning achievement, albeit one that was somewhat overlooked in the wake of the attack on Nancy.

By contrast, Nancy's dream of star status took much longer to realize, despite a steady stream of successes. She won regularly and was widely recognized as a skater with considerable potential, but so were plenty of others. Theresa Martin was very comfortable with the pace of Nancy's development. "We looked at it as a long career," Martin said. "Every year we would sit down and ask, 'What do you want to accomplish this year?' When she met that goal, we'd go on from there."

By the time Nancy was in her early teens,

skating was consuming virtually all of her time away from school and a like amount of the family's resources. Dan Kerrigan would make the predawn trips to the rink, then stay around to make a few extra bucks by driving the rink's Zamboni machine. He also refinanced the house a few times and found extra work whenever possible. The cost of instruction, ice time, skates, outfits, and travel can easily run into twenty-five to thirty thousand dollars per year for an aspiring national-level competitor.

When a family is making sacrifices of this magnitude, it's only natural for questions to arise from time to time about where the whole thing is headed. Brenda Kerrigan would occasionally talk to Nancy's instructors, asking, "Do you think this is worth it? Are we crazy to do all this running around and getting up early?" In truth, the skating-centric life-style may have been harder on Brenda Kerrigan than anyone, because her deteriorating vision made it increasingly difficult for her to fully appreciate her daughter's talent. A viral disease began afflicting Brenda Kerrigan in 1970, the year after Nancy was born. It progressively attacked the nerves around her eyes to the point that she became legally blind. "Sometimes if I stand real close, I can see [Nancy when she is skating]," Brenda told the *Boston*

Globe in 1991. "In years past, I could go to the rink and tell what was going on. Now if I sit in the stands, I would miss all of the performance. I don't know how to explain what I see. I can hear—my ears are good. But words don't tell me what I see.

"I never see her hand. I never see her face," Brenda told *Newsweek* at Detroit in 1994. "I would do anything to see her. There are times when I say, 'Come here. I just want to look at you.' We get nose to nose, and I try to see what everyone else sees in her." Even nose to nose, the image never gets much better than fuzzy. The frustration can be immense, but by all accounts Brenda Kerrigan has battled it admirably. In the familiar surroundings of their home, she navigates comfortably and, outside of cooking, which her husband takes care of, performs much of the business of daily life. She even has been known to go bowling, skiing, and aerobic dancing. She remains as independent as the affliction will allow.

An effervescent woman with short, reddish-blond hair, Brenda Kerrigan also has the comfort of knowing her daughter is very committed to helping on a larger scale. In 1993 Nancy became honorary chairperson for a campaign called SightFirst, a global effort sponsored by Lions Club International seeking to raise $130 million for treatment of reversible blindness.

Nancy is helping to publicize the fact that by World Health Organization (WHO) estimates, forty million suffer from blindness that could have been prevented.

"My mom has always been my biggest fan," Nancy said shortly after joining the campaign. "She has never allowed her blindness to stop her from enjoying life. But for many, blindness is a devastating reality that represents a tremendous loss of human productivity and an enormous social burden."

&

Any questions or doubts that may have popped up about Nancy's skating ultimately were short-lived. She wasn't one of these overburdened teenagers we've seen too often, the young athlete who becomes so obsessed with "making it" that she loses all sense of joy, the very thing that drew her to the sport in the first place. Nancy loved skating. She loved competing. And she was attracting more and more attention as a young figure skater on the rise. Ducky Antonucci, who was watching Nancy Kerrigan at age six, was not surprised.

"She always had the drive to go where she is today," Antonucci said. "The farther she got, the more she wanted to stay with it. She just had this special natural talent, and she worked very hard to develop it."

"She has that positive and hopeful trait in her personality that she can do anything," Evy Scotvold said in an interview with *Skating* magazine. "She's not afraid of anything. The only thing that can stand in her way is herself. Most us have a few roadblocks, but she doesn't."

Three

Going National

By the time she gets to the ice for most major competitions, Nancy Kerrigan has usually received a fresh bouquet of blue and gold flowers, along with a note of encouragement. The flowers are done in her old school colors. They are a gift from Sister Janet Eisner, president of Emmanuel College in Boston. Located a few corners from Fenway Park, Emmanuel was the first Catholic women's college in New England. It was where Kerrigan earned her associate degree in business studies. The school is obviously quite proud of this association: in its promotional material it makes passing reference to the numerous distinguished professionals and executives it has turned out, but by name mentions only one alumna—figure skater Nancy Kerrigan.

It made perfect sense for Kerrigan to attend college close to home. Apart from wanting to stay near her family, this allowed her to continue to put in her monster training hours with the Scotvolds at their rink in nearby Cape Cod. Nor did it hurt that the tiny school, with an average class size of twelve students, was flexible about accommodating the demands of her skating.

Kerrigan was newly enrolled at Emmanuel when she began edging into the national elite. In 1988 she won the New England Senior competition, then the National Collegiates, an event put on by the USFSA. She successfully defended her New England crown the following year, when she also won the eastern title and captured third in the World University Games.

Her progress continued to be steady, if unspectacular, as it had been for years. If anybody was getting restless about that, there were certainly no outward indications. Wise, seasoned hands at developing skaters, Evy and Mary Scotvold were not about to risk Nancy's future by putting the pedal to the proverbial metal. What would be the point? She was coming very nicely. She was right where she needed to be.

Undeniably, Nancy's biggest breakthrough to this point came at the U.S. Olympic Festival in Minneapolis in July of 1990. On a sunny and unseasonably warm day, Kerrigan squared off against a diminutive, thickly muscled jumping machine from Portland, Oregon, named Tonya Harding. Harding's dazzling jumps had long been her trademark, and now the word was that she would be trying to take a leap into history by becoming the first American woman to do a triple axel. Though Harding trailed Kerrigan after the short program, she was widely expected to jump her way to the gold medal in the long program. Kerrigan, for her part, refused to get caught up in any of the jumping mania. In fact, she didn't even plan to watch Harding's long program. "It doesn't matter what they do. It doesn't matter how good they are," she said of her opponents. "I just have to do what I can do."

Harding wound up spending as much time sprawling as jumping. She fell on the triple axel and on two other triple jumps as well. Kerrigan was the last of the six skaters to come on. Wearing a dramatic white outfit with gold beads, long sleeves, and an open back, she looked like a bride on blades. She took the ice knowing the gold was well within her grasp.

Before a sellout crowd of close to fifteen thousand people, Kerrigan was a picture of poise and elegance, her dark hair accentuated by all the white, her skating strong and graceful. She didn't try to duplicate Harding's daring, but that was never the plan. Kerrigan's performance was not flawless; she touched her hand down on a triple flip jump and again on a triple lutz. But it was plenty good enough to the judges, all seven of whom rated her the winner.

"It's fun because I did well, and it's an important tournament for me," Kerrigan said. "I haven't won a big competition at the senior level. What's important now is to concentrate on what I can do and do it more consistently. I just want to go back to work to make sure I can do it again." After gaining the silver medal, Harding, who would soon succeed in pulling off the triple axel, said her only problem on this day was that she got too close to the side wall. "I fell three times—it's quite an honor to finish second," Harding said.

There was more good fortune not long after Nancy left Minneapolis. She got a call from the USFSA. Holly Cook, who was third in the 1990 World Championships, was unable to compete in the Goodwill Games the following month in Seattle. A replacement was needed pronto, and with the added incentive of an appearance fee from the organizers, Kerrigan agreed.

Not that it wasn't a daunting prospect. The field at the Goodwill Games was by far the strongest Nancy had ever been in. Jill Trenary, three-time national champion and reigning world champion, would be there. So would Kristi Yamaguchi, who had won the festival title the previous year and for two years had been runner-up to Trenary in the nationals. Also in the competition was a sixteen-year-old French girl, Surya Bonaly, whose acrobatic jumps and back flips had made her something of an international wunderkind.

After just a few weeks of preparation, Nancy headed west. In the first part of the competition, things went splendidly. Nancy was second after the original program, behind Trenary and ahead of Yamaguchi. With a strong, long program, she would be a lock for a medal and for a huge step forward onto the world stage. Nancy came on after both Trenary and Yamaguchi had finished their long programs. It was all right there for her.

And then, suddenly, it wasn't.

To call her performance a disappointment would not be accurate: it amounted to a prime-time meltdown. She kept falling down. She could get no rhythm, no confidence. They were four of the longest minutes of her skating career.

"She was probably not ready for the position that she was in at the Goodwill Games," Evy Scotvold told the *Boston Globe* later. "She wanted to beat Jill and Kristi instead of focusing on what she does. Sometimes skaters get carried away with trying to outdo one another instead of concentrating on their own program.

"What happened in the Goodwill Games was traumatic," the coach continued. "A lot of people think Nancy is more experienced than she really is. But she has not been to half the internationals, she has never been on tour, and those are tremendous guides."

It was hard for Nancy not to agree. "I heard Jill's marks right before going out there, and I started thinking too much," she said in a *Skating* magazine interview. "I thought, This is unbelievable. I'm not even supposed to be here. I had it physically, but my mind messed it up."

The cleanup of the emotional wreckage began immediately. Nancy immersed herself once more in training. The Scotvolds worked almost as much on the mental aspect as they did the physical. Kerrigan heard plenty about "when the going gets tough" and similar themes. She heard about how champions are decided not by who falls, but by who's the best at getting up. The Scotvolds may have risked sounding like Vince Lombardi wannabes, but it worked. Kerrigan took a hard look at her Goodwill Games performance. As she told a reporter later, "[It] was bad because I kind of just let it snowball. I fell once and couldn't let it go. I just let it keep distracting me as I skated."

This phenomenon is what Kerrigan's training partner and close friend, Paul Wylie, calls "the Voice." It is as insidious as it is widespread among figure skaters. Doubts set in, harsh self-judgments set in, and before long the isolated "Voice" is more like an angry mob. It robs the skater of what may be his or her most critical faculty: total concentration.

The Scotvolds did not have long to wait to find out how fully Kerrigan had absorbed their message. The opportunity came the following February 1991, in the U.S. National Championships at the Target Center in Minneapolis, not far from the site of Kerrigan's triumph in the Olympic Festival the year before. Harding stole nearly all of the headlines by winning the gold medal, landing her historic triple axel and earning the first perfect 6.0 score for technical merit by an American woman in close to twenty years. "I just went out and did what I wanted to do," Harding said matter-of-factly. But Nancy Kerrigan was no less heartened by her own performance. On the first jump of her long program, she muffed a basic double and tumbled to the ice. It amounted to a personal, highly public crucible. Would she able to put the mistake behind her? Could she silence the Voice and free herself simply to skate?

The answer came barely three minutes later, when the ten thousand–plus Target Center fans gave Kerrigan a standing ovation. Except for a triple flip that became a double, she had skated the balance of her program beautifully, as if the start had belonged to somebody else.

"I told myself, 'You've trained for this. You can fix what you've done,'" Kerrigan said to the *Globe*. "I fought back and ended up skating a good program."

Calling it "a tremendous boost in confidence for Nancy," Evy Scotvold said, "It showed her that she had the talent, the material, and the flair and that the judges recognized her. It also showed her that she could deal with problems, block them out, and just skate."

The performance earned Kerrigan third place, right behind Harding and Yamaguchi, her highest finish ever in the nationals. It also qualified her for the World Championships, to be held the following month in Munich's Olympiahalle. There, too, Kerrigan overcame an early slip-up and went on to skate superbly, earning a bronze medal in her first appearance in the worlds. To secure the medal, Kerrigan edged Japan's Midori Ito, who came in as everybody's favorite for the gold but wound up victim of an ill-timed bout of ice follies.

In warm-ups prior to the short program, Ito crashed into another skater, a collision that left Ito with bruised ribs, slumped in a heap against the sideboards with tears running down her cheeks. When she resumed her warm-up, she almost sailed into the boards again after landing a combination jump. The short program itself was not that much better, as Ito, a fast-spinning jumper and the first woman to land a triple axel, actually skated off the ice for a moment after a triple-double combination. There was a foot-high barrier along the boards, right in front of a television camera. Ito skidded off and back on, and though she wound up with marks good enough to place third, she couldn't hold on in the long program. With her ribs and ankle hurting so badly that she was unsure she could compete, Ito landed only half of her eight triple jumps. (It may be that the only reason she even tried so hard to hold on to third was the knowledge that if she succeeded, Japan would thus be able to send three skaters to the Olympics.)

Kerrigan's solidly graceful effort to win the bronze was but one highlight of a momentous night for the American women, who pulled off a gold-silver-bronze sweep; it was the only time in the history of the event, which began in 1924, that women from the same country had taken all the medals. The unquestioned star of the night was Yamaguchi, the nineteen-year-old from Fremont, California, who did some solo record setting, too, scoring the first 6.0 for artistic impression the championships had ever had. Yamaguchi had been working feverishly to come up with a triple axel to match those of her rivals Harding and Ito, but to no avail. As it turned out, she did not need it—not with her artful, dazzling display and with Harding unable to nail her jumps the way she had hoped.

For Nancy Kerrigan, her triumphant showing in Munich in March 1991 was that much more meaningful after the stinging memory of the previous year, when a tearful Kerrigan had watched the World Championships from Halifax, Nova Scotia, on a television set. On her screen was Paul Wylie. She was thrilled for Paul and miserable for herself. "I wanted to be there, too," she said.

Kerrigan wasn't there because the month before in Salt Lake City, at the U.S. National Championships, she had finished a fraction behind bronze medalist Holly Cook. Actually, after Kerrigan finished her long program, she seemed well positioned to stay in third, so much so that Yamaguchi, with whom she'd become very close over the years, rushed over to congratulate her for making the team. Moments later Cook's scores were on the board and Nancy Kerrigan was the fourth member of a three-person U.S. world team. She was so upset at the emotional whiplash that she briefly lashed out at Yamaguchi for falsely raising her hopes.

The sting was subsequently erased by winning the gold medal at the Olympic Festival several months later, in the summer of 1990. And it was ancient history by the end of 1991, when Nancy Kerrigan, a World Championships bronze medalist, was poised on the brink of a dream she'd had almost from the time she'd showed up in a blue dress and tears at Theresa Martin's skating class at Stoneham Arena. The 1992 U.S. National Championships were fast approaching. Another top three finish would mean that Nancy Kerrigan would be a member of the United States Olympic team and would compete in the Winter Games in Albertville, France. She could hardly wait, and neither could most of Stoneham.

Four

Bronze in the Alps

The American sweep of the 1991 World Championships in Munich was even more remarkable given that it was achieved without Jill Trenary, the defending world champion and three-time U.S. national champion. Trenary, of Minnetonka, Minnesota, sat it out because she was recuperating from ankle surgery at the U.S. Olympic Committee training center in Colorado Springs. Not long after Yamaguchi, Harding, and Kerrigan made their history, Trenary received a phone call from *Sports Illustrated,* seeking her reaction. "I think it's wonderful," she said. "It means next year's nationals is going to be like the Olympics."

She was not far wrong. The 1992 U.S. Figure Skating Championships, in Orlando, Florida, figured to be the hottest attraction since Mickey Mouse and Donald Duck hit town. Not only would it determine who would be going to the Olympics, it would feature a veritable Who's Who of figure-skating champions. The field was expected to include two world champions (Trenary and Yamaguchi) one defending national champion (Harding) and a pair of world bronze medalists (Holly Cook and Nancy Kerrigan). Has there ever been a single national competition so stacked with talent? Probably not.

Ultimately, the murderer's row lineup did not fully materialize. Still on the mend from her injury, Trenary apparently felt this was too tough a field to take on and decided to retire. Holly Cook, the woman who nosed Kerrigan out of the third spot for the 1990 worlds, also took a pass. Even with the dropouts, the competition promised to be intense. Apart from Yamaguchi, Harding, and Kerrigan, a couple of new kids, Tonia Kwiatkowski and Lisa Ervin—both coached by 1960 Olympic gold medalist Carol Heiss Jenkins—were threatening a major breakthrough. When a reporter asked Kerrigan if the U.S. skaters could pull off another sweep at the Olympics, she said, "I don't know if it can happen twice, but it would be pretty exciting."

The competition was pretty exciting itself. Yamaguchi had a world championship to her credit but had never won a national title in her four years as a senior, finishing as runner-up three consecutive years. She took care of that convincingly enough, capturing the top scores from all nine judges both in the original and long programs. Almost as gratifying as the gold to Yamaguchi was that she was able to land a triple salchow jump for the first time in more than a year. In a salchow, the skater takes off from the back inside edge of one foot and lands on the back outside of the other foot. "I was most excited about that jump," she said. "Coming into competition, I said no matter what I do, I'm going to land that triple salchow." In case anybody doubted her elation, the lithe little skater emphatically pumped her fist after pulling off the jump.

Nancy Kerrigan was not quite up to the standards of Yamaguchi, who landed seven triple jumps and received a 6.0 score for composition and style, but she nonetheless impressed the judges with her usual elegance and grace. It was becoming clear that Kerrigan's artistry and style were fast improving, to the point where there were few skaters in the world not named Yamaguchi who could match her in those areas. "When she is skating well, she is so beautiful to watch," Evy Scotvold said. "Maybe she needed to convince herself of that, and I think that happened [with her great strides forward in 1991]." Kerrigan could sense the evolution herself. "I had no style when I was a young skater," she said. "When I was little, I was a spaz. All I could do was go back and forth and up and down the ice real fast." All along she has credited the Scotvolds for teaching her the nuances of style. "Now I have more of a concept of where I'm supposed to be and how I get to do what I do," she said.

"Spaz" was not a word on anybody's lips at Orlando Arena, not after Kerrigan's performance earned her the silver medal, ahead of Tonya Harding's bronze. She got a warm ovation from the crowd. She had won over a lot of people still unaccustomed to seeing her at this high a level. Most important of all, she was an Olympian. The sense of relief she felt was immense.

Throughout the championships, no matter how much Kerrigan tried to downplay it in her own mind, it was impossible not to realize what was at stake. A career that had begun sixteen years ago had come down to this, 240 seconds of skating, with millions of people around the country watching. If she wanted to go to the

Olympics, she had to produce, here and now. She had to keep the Voice from making any unscheduled appearances and screwing up everything.

Even after she was on the medal stand, waving to the appreciative crowd, Kerrigan was having a hard time letting it sink in. The thought kept dancing in her mind: I'm going to the Olympics. How could she even begin to comprehend that? The sinking-in process was helped along after the plane trip home to Logan International Airport. Kerrigan drifted off to sleep during the flight. When she woke up and walked through the tunnel into the terminal, cheers and hugs and welcome-home signs were being waved by family, friends, and fellow Emmanuel students. "There's just a lot of pressure to make the team, and now that I have, a little bit of pressure is off my back," she told reporters. "I can relax and go have fun and maybe get off a better program than the last one."

The news that Nancy was heading to France buzzed through Stoneham faster than you can say *"Bonjour."* The *Stoneham Independent* dug into its archives. It discovered that the town had produced six Olympians, including a figure skater, Nancy Rouillard Graham, who competed in the pairs competition in Squaw Valley in 1960. But nothing compared with this. Dave's Place, the tidy little breakfast joint, was hopping with Kerrigan talk, as was Hank's Bakery and, probably more than any place in town, Stoneham Arena.

"We knew she was a national figure, but it still came as a slight surprise to a lot of people that she was going to the Olympics," said Jeff Gutridge, editor of the *Independent*. "She was always in our paper for winning competitions. I had been doing my usual stories on the front page [for years]. But she was never really a major figure in town until we found out she was going. Having someone on the Olympic team was probably the biggest thing of all. Grabbing a medal was actually secondary."

The scope of the Olympics was staggering. The crush of traffic, reporters, and fans clogged every inch of Albertville. Everywhere you went there was a mix of commotion and excitement, the unmistakable charge that courses through a place that's hosting such a global extravaganza. The athletes' foremost task—particularly for figure skaters, who are under as much scrutiny as any competitors in the games—is to block out all the peripheral stuff. Get into a comfortable routine. Eat right, go to the rink for practice, get some sleep—the more basic the life-style, the better.

A huge help to Nancy was having Kristi Yamaguchi as a roommate. They had gotten to be good friends from years of competing against each other. They had similar outlooks on things. Both were unpretentious, unassuming young women who loved where the skating world had taken them but were not altogether comfortable in the spotlight. Answering endless questions, feeling the unrelenting weight of being watched—it was a lot to deal with. While they were in Albertville, somebody actually demanded an answer to one burning question: Who's the neat one and who's the messy one? The wonder was that nobody wrote stories about who left the cap off the toothpaste.

When Yamaguchi opted to turn pro after the Albertville games, she said that "one of the toughest things about this decision was knowing I'd be leaving Nancy. Having Nancy has always been a comfort zone for me. I know that she'll be okay and do very well without me. I'd like very much for her to succeed me as world champion."

Paul Wylie was also in Albertville, and before he delivered the performance of his life to capture the silver medal, he was a major positive influence on Kerrigan, too. At twenty-seven, Wylie was five years Nancy's senior and an Olympic veteran, and his big-brotherly advice helped her keep things in perspective. A bright, sensitive man, Wylie knew it would be silly simply to tell Kerrigan to calm down and not let things get to her. He offered concrete suggestions: Get a Walkman and listen to music she liked. Train her mind to think positive, soothing thoughts. Take steps to be in control, to avoid the Alpine madness swirling around her. And he didn't stop there. He also joined her at press conferences, practices, even other events around town.

"What I did was make her feel that anything was possible," Wylie said.

Just as helpful as having Yamaguchi and Wylie around her, according to Evy Svotvold, was a three-day bout with the flu shortly after she arrived. Rather than running the risk of overtraining or getting flat as she waited for the competition to begin, Kerrigan rested and took care of the bug.

In any case, Kerrigan went out in the original program and didn't seem fazed in the least that she was in the Olympics. After the original scores were tallied, she was in second place, trailing only Yamaguchi. Kerrigan said later that it was almost as if she were skating for friends at home. "It was fun," she said. "It was just a lot easier than the time when you're thinking too much about how you've got to do it."

The original program is worth one-third of a skater's total score, the long program two-thirds. Kerrigan was well positioned to win a medal, particularly since the unquestioned favorite to win the gold—Midori Ito—fell while attempting a relatively routine triple combination in her short program. Ito wound up in fourth place, two ahead of Tonya Harding, who got unraveled on a triple axel combination and took a spill of her own.

As the four-minute-long program commenced two days later, it was clear that Yamaguchi would've had to thoroughly collapse not to capture the gold. Nobody expected that to happen. While falling short of the flowing artistry of her short program, Yamaguchi nonetheless gave a commanding performance. She was a ninety-three-pound wonder, with a feathery touch and style both athletic and ethereal. Even with a slip-up on a triple loop, she had the crowd totally captivated.

Yamaguchi skated first in the final group of skaters. Soon it was Nancy Kerrigan's turn. She skated out into the middle of the spanking new, white arena, receiving a nice ovation. She glided into her routine. Kerrigan missed a combination and singled two of the triple jumps she had planned to do, but she stayed with it, just as she did when she momentarily touched down on a triple toe loop. There was every opportunity for a repeat of the Goodwill Games in 1990, when she'd lost it completely, but she refused to give in. "I wasn't thinking about being perfect," she said later. "I was just thinking about presenting my program and letting whatever would happen [happen]."

Surya Bonaly, who was in third place after the short program, skated without much artistry and didn't even jump particularly well; she fell into fifth place. Harding improved over her short program but wasn't going to get into medal territory, either. That left Midori Ito, who had virtually no shot to catch Yamaguchi. Ito encountered difficulty early in her program when she fell on her first triple axel. To her everlasting credit, she carried on even after that disappointment and ended her program magnificently, the highlight being a second, perfectly executed triple axel. Her late rally earned her the silver medal and great respect among skaters and fans alike. She had come into the games with the oppressive burden of an entire nation's expectations, and you could almost see her progressively crumbling under it as the week went by. She's a popular, industrious, hugely talented skater. People were happy to see her come back. Writer E. M. Swift of *Sports Illustrated* went so far as to call her successful triple axel possibly "the single gutsiest moment of the figure-skating competition."

As the last skater finished, spontaneous American celebrations erupted all over the arena. People waved flags, sung songs, and screamed in delight to the heroines on the ice. Thanks to the performances of Kristi Yamaguchi, gold medalist, and Nancy Kerrigan of Stoneham, Massachusetts, the 1992 Olympic bronze medalist, the United States placed two women on the Olympic medal platform for the first time since 1960, when Carol Heiss won the gold and Barbara Ann Roles the bronze. And Harding's fourth-place finish made it the finest American finish in Olympic history.

At the medal ceremony, a bashful Yamaguchi looked as if she didn't know what to say or do. Kerrigan smiled and nodded to her and gave her a tender little nudge to get up on the platform. "I've dreamed of this since I was a little girl putting on skates for the first time," Yamaguchi said.

Kerrigan was deep in revelry of her own. She didn't try to hide her disappointment about a few of the mistakes she had made, but how could she argue with the results? Four years ago Nancy Kerrigan had been ranked number twelve in the country. Now she was third in the world. "I'm definitely satisfied with my placement," she said. "Some things I was very pleased with. Others could have gone better.

"It feels wonderful to have the gold medal," she said. "This is a tough group to compete against."

Not far away, Brenda Kerrigan, who had watched the competition with her husband on a television monitor provided by CBS, tried to fight back tears. She talked about how overwhelmed she was. Brenda wasn't sure Nancy's performance was going to be enough to get a medal. Moments after Nancy had finished, Brenda hugged her and told her she loved her. When Brenda was told about the final standings, it was all too much. Where was all the emotion supposed to go at a time like that? Had anybody ever died from too much joy? How could Dan and Brenda Kerrigan not remember what it had cost all of them—from the four-thirty wake-up calls and the thousands of dollars to the dedication of a little girl whose life revolved around a rink—and how it had paid off at last, in immeasurable pride and joy?

Evy and Mary Scotvold couldn't help but think back, too, about how far their pupil had come, how right they'd been not to rush her. As Evy told the *Globe,* "In less than twelve months Nancy gets two bronze medals—the worlds and the Olympics. And that ain't bad."

Soon all of Stoneham was in on the celebration. The Sunday after Nancy Kerrigan returned with her bronze medal, forty thousand people turned out for a welcome-home parade. The *Independent* called it the biggest party in the town's 267-year history. Who could argue?

Nancy was wearing a red, white, and blue Olympic jacket and a headband. Every time she smiled it seemed to send people into a frenzy. She was riding in the back of a green convertible. The car went about one mile per hour because of all the well-wishers and picture takers. Who knows how long it took to cover the 1.6-mile route from Stoneham High School to Stoneham Arena? There were marching bands, fire departments, Shriner Units, and the Ancient and Honorary Artillery Company, just to be certain Nancy didn't get lonely. On top of McDonough's Liquors in Stoneham Square, in the middle of downtown, kids were holding up signs with the number 6.0, the perfect figure-skating score. Nancy Kerrigan hadn't rung up any of those, but nobody cared about the revisionist history. This was a party, not an accounting class. One young skater, a ten-year-old named Kelsey Thayer from nearby Reading, said, "Oh, God, I just died. I touched her. I talked to her. She has inspired me."

When the convertible finally reached the arena, they had a Nancy Kerrigan Welcome Home Social. The $10 tickets were sold out within half an hour. They had more tributes, and Nancy kept smiling and waving, expressing her thanks. The roof all but came down when she took a spin around the ice.

Ducky Antonucci, Stoneham's veteran skating teacher, said the whole day would be a hard one for anybody to forget. "The town of Stoneham has been right behind her the whole way," she said. "People everywhere love Nancy."

Five

Ascending to
the Throne

*The U.S. National Championships,
January 1993, Phoenix, Arizona*

In figure skating, the top woman is the star, the franchise, generating a maelstrom of attention. In this sport, finally, the women run the workplace. They are the last to skate, because they are the most important. "They are the show," said Claire Ferguson, president of the U.S. Figure Skating Association. Men can spin faster, jump higher. But they cannot be Sonja Henie, Peggy Fleming, Dorothy Hamill, or Nancy Kerrigan. This is ballet and theater, not just sport.

Traditionally, women skaters have shorter shelf lives than men. Like actresses, they have difficulty finding respectable roles once they hit twenty-five. This creates an accelerated biological clock and a very real sense of limited opportunity. For Nancy Kerrigan, Phoenix was the official opening of her window of opportunity. She was now the star, until the Lillehammer Olympics. Yamaguchi was off on the professional circuit, touring with the Discovery show and finding that it was more fun to dance to hip-hop music than to practice a demanding program over and over. Midori Ito, the silver medalist at Albertville, also had retired from demanding amateur competition. Yamaguchi would flirt with the idea of returning to the Olympics in 1994; but by April 1993, the deadline for reinstatement and eligibility, she had given up the idea. As the defending gold medalist, Yamaguchi was making good money with her exhibitions. Already, however, she was getting outendorsed by Kerrigan in the corporate world.

Kerrigan was the darling of the sponsors and the television cameras, for obvious reasons. Here was the whole package: the face of Katharine Hepburn, with high cheekbones, pouty lips, and elegant eyes; gritty, devoted parents; a graceful beauty who could also jump. As she arrived in Phoenix, however, Kerrigan also happened to be a nervous wreck. She was not doing well, adjusting to the role of favorite. She was wringing her hands at press conferences and pressing too hard in practice.

This did not seem to matter to major corporate sponsors, who were too busy throwing money at her, too busy demanding her time, to notice her frailties. Her royal predecessor, Yamaguchi, had been unable to land major American sponsors until DuraSoft finally came to her aid. Yamaguchi would never admit that her commercial opportunities were limited because she was an Asian-American; that would have been financial suicide. But Kerrigan, a mere bronze medalist, already was a spokeswoman for Visa, Reebock, Evian, Northwest Airlines, Campbell's soup, and Seiko watches. She was involved with a dozen other endorsements, local and national, earning in the high six figures annually. To Kerrigan, this was all very lucrative but a bit distracting and confusing. She was far more comfortable at home in Stoneham, Massachusetts, or at her rink, signing autographs for the kids who adored her. She adored them, too. They reminded her of herself a few years back. Before the fuss.

The money and the attention were necessary, even desirable, Kerrigan understood. Never again would she have to worry about training funds or her family's future. Her parents no longer had to make huge financial sacrifices. But because the big money was so new to her, because she had come from a working-class family with strong ethics, Kerrigan felt she had to earn her wages. And she couldn't figure out how.

"I don't really know what they want me to say," Kerrigan said about her role as Seiko spokesperson. She seemed genuinely concerned.

Nobody was asking Kerrigan to say much. She was too shy for that. Instead, her job was to skate flawlessly and to mount the medal stand, smiling, in full pulchritude, in her hot-pink Lycra outfit designed by Wang. Sponsors would do the rest, complete the picture. Kerrigan tried to say the right things, wear the right clothes and bangles. Her outfits were a hot topic. Would she wear the black Wang in her technical program or the white one? It wasn't always easy being front and center. Kerrigan was told to relax at press conferences, to be more forthcoming. She hadn't learned yet to filter her thoughts for public consumption. When a reporter asked her about the possible Olympic comeback of Katarina Witt, the two-time champion circa 1988, Kerrigan nearly laughed out loud at the concept of a woman from the three-triple era competing in the five-triple era. "I don't think so," Kerrigan said.

Unfortunately for Seiko and the other companies, Kerrigan was not a sure thing, not like Yamaguchi. Her long program was a real minefield. She had not skated it successfully since 1991, and she had not put in the practice hours that were needed to do so. There were so many commercials to film and appearances to make. Any triple jump was going to be risky business in Phoenix.

Kerrigan's supporters believed, correctly, that their skater could survive a tumble at the nationals. Her technical and long programs, so carefully constructed to highlight her grace and line, would outclass the others. She was guaranteed to earn 5.9's on artistic merit from the judges. Poor technical marks would be embarrassing, but not fatal.

As it turned out, Kerrigan's undoing in Phoenix was the triple lutz, the most difficult jump in her long program. She fell on that one, then abandoned two other planned triples, careening way off form. It didn't matter. This was her turn, and her competitors were just as bad, maybe worse. Kerrigan was awarded first place anyway and sent off to the worlds in Prague as America's standard-bearer.

"This is the chance I've been waiting for," Kerrigan said. "I like to think I'm going to take advantage of it."

While Kerrigan's top placement was expected, nothing else about the championships in Phoenix was predictable. Figure skating was at a crazy crossroads, with the impending turn of professionals and the growing scandals from within. Brian Boitano, Katarina Witt, Jayne Torvill, and Christopher Dean were banging at the door again. The world was changing too fast.

There were those nasty reports about AIDS. Four world-class figure skaters and several coaches and choreographers had died recently of the societal plague. In Canada, Dennis Coi, Rob McCall, and Brian Pockar, all national championship caliber, had been victims. John Curry, the brilliant Olympic champion from Great Britain, was nearly dead from the disease, living his final days in exile, turning away sympathy calls and requests for interviews. There were coaches, choreographers, trainers, judges, all dead or dying. The figure-skating community held a benefit in Toronto for McCall, a benefit in England for Curry, but was clearly confused about its position on the issue.

On the one hand, there was no disguising the deadly toll. Journalists could count bodies. But there was great concern about spooking potential sponsors on the issue. One USFSA member estimated that the association had lost about $500,000 in endorsements in three months since the problem became a subject of the national press. The tabloid TV shows jumped in, quickly. Sponsors were edgy, and figure-skating officials were very busy protecting them. After an official from L'eggs announced his company's multimillion-dollar sponsorship of figure skating at a press conference with Ferguson, he found himself escorted briskly off the dais. The line of questioning from reporters had turned to AIDS. Kerrigan and the women had become easier, safer athletes to sponsor than the men or the sport as a whole.

The issue went beyond the disease, of course; it touched on the delicate question of homosexuality in the sport. For decades, figure skating had been sold easily to middle America in a tidy, Ice Capades package. It was, in truth, a glorious sport, an agile, story-telling circus act on concave, rocking chair blades the width of three millimeters. There were such endearing celebrities, too: Fleming, Hamill, Scott Hamilton. Solid family fun, a slippery tightrope act, with a triple axel thrown in for thrills. Figure-skating exhibitions drew phenomenal television ratings, whether the skaters were performing live or on tape from some obscure competition four months earlier.

Now, officials feared, the very status of the sport was at risk with this skittish audience.

Even the Kerrigans might be affected, by extension. Everybody understood that the percentage of gay male skaters in figure skating was relatively higher than that in any other sport, perhaps comparable to the statistics from the theater or dance worlds. And almost everybody believed that such publicity would be box office poison.

"We're spending hours every day discussing this thing at USFSA meetings, and nobody knows what to do," said Bonnie McLauthlin, a sixty-two-year-old judge from Denver who had seen, and heard, almost everything.

Athletes wanted to steer a wide berth around the issue. AIDS activism was not a marketable gold medallion. When Craig McQueen, chairman of the USFSA sports medicine committee, held a widely publicized seminar in Phoenix on AIDS, not a single figure skater showed. Brian Boitano, usually a perceptive, honest interview, was one of the absentees. He played good soldier on the AIDS issue.

"People die of AIDS everywhere, not just in figure skating," Boitano said. "Every sport probably has the same problem. The vast majority of skaters in this sport are straight."

The sport's obsession with image, and with marketing, had driven it into borderline homophobia. Virtually every male figure skater, gay and straight, found it necessary to present himself in some sort of boastful heterosexual pose. At press conferences and in private conversations with journalists, Mark Mitchell spoke often about his girlfriend; Viktor Petrenko about his wife, the daughter of his coach; Paul Wylie about his fiancée.

To some degree, the figure-skating world actually policed itself on the sexual front. Scoring marks became subjective, prudish weapons in the hands of a nine-member jury of judges. The judges were not so petty as to penalize suspected gay skaters, but they punished a few stray athletes who were perceived to have gone overboard with their behavioral exploits. Once, these same judges had enforced economic and political ideologies, defending international borders with intense jingoism. Judges from the West downgraded the Soviets. Soviet judges returned the favor, on behalf of the communist order. Now the Cold War was over, but a greater moral struggle was at hand. American skaters were being observed, and tried, at all hours of the day, by American judges and team officials. When the athletes practiced, the judges watched carefully, rinkside, to learn of any new technical moves the skaters might be developing as secret weapons. When the skaters partied, team leaders and monitors were on hand to act as societal spies. "They are everywhere, watching me," said

Jaclyn Ward, a fifteen-year-old juniors skater. "Kristi Yamaguchi had to work hard, twenty-four hours a day, to maintain her squeaky-clean image. Now, I can appreciate how hard it was for her."

Under these circumstances, the USFSA was infinitely more comfortable with Kerrigan than it would have been with her chief rival, Tonya Harding Gillooly. Kerrigan was "a good girl" by anybody's definition. She kept her private life private. When she became engaged to a hometown accountant soon after the Phoenix championships, the ring on her finger was a surprise to almost everybody. The man in question was known only as "Billy" to the figure-skating community. When the engagement was broken off a few months later, she wouldn't talk about it. There were rumors that she was dating Michael Collins, son of tour promoter Tom Collins. But, again, Kerrigan politely declined to discuss the matter.

Harding, on the other hand, was something of a public embarrassment. She had fired many coaches, survived many marital spats, on her way up the ladder. Her last name changed almost annually, depending on whether or not she still considered herself married. In Phoenix, the "Gillooly" made an unhyphenated return, as her husband paced nervously in the gallery. Harding took chances on the ice—

crazy, suicidal triple jumps of fancy that almost always ended badly sooner or later. She had been the first American woman to complete a triple axel in competition, at the 1991 nationals. That was the way she lived, always on the outside edge. In Phoenix, Harding and her coaches tried so hard to be normal, happy folks, they had to laugh a bit at themselves.

"We're just like the Cleaver family," said Diane Rawlinson, Harding's on-again, off-again coach.

The happy veneer was not deep. Harding remained fragile on many topics, very sensitive about her weight problems. By normal standards she was a slim, athletic woman, a blue-eyed beauty. In the world of figure skating, which rivals ballet in its low-body-fat demands, Harding bordered on obese. For the nationals she had clearly lost some weight, but Harding would not say how much or how she had gone about it. She was clearly embarrassed, deferring these questions to Rawlinson.

"Did she lose any of her energy when she lost her weight?" asked Julie Vader, a columnist from Portland's *Oregonian*.

"No, she did it very carefully, with Jenny Craig," Rawlinson said.

At this disclosure, Harding walked to a corner and began to cry. It was as if a parent had said something terribly embarrassing about a teenage daughter during an adult party. This was not such a happy camper, after all.

On top of her self-conscious weight battle in Phoenix, Harding suffered from chronic asthma, allergies to all flowers except roses, the flu, and a clear death wish. Proof positive: despite all her respiratory problems, Harding was known to sneak the occasional cigarette.

The blueprint for Harding's long program was, again, nearly impossible, laced with several tough combinations and a triple axel. These feats of daring were bound to unhinge her. Nobody could quite figure out why she or Rawlinson continued to outline such an ambitious routine, when a far simpler one, if done correctly, would assure her second place and a trip to the World Championships.

In fact, when the time came, Harding backed off the triple axel. She fell on a triple loop, a slightly simpler jump with both takeoff and landing on the back outside edge. Then, just as her music peaked, Harding stepped out of a triple loop in midflight. A disaster, but not the only one. Harding, somehow, was dropped to fourth place, behind fifteen-year-old Lisa Ervin and the older Tonia Kwiatkowski. She would not go to Prague. "It's not fair," said one judge, watching ladies' competition after judging the men's. "If they're going to let Tonya skate, they have to give her the scores."

Harding wheezed herself off the ice as familiar tears welled in her eyes. Because of the antidrug zealotry of the International Olympic Committee, Harding was not permitted to take an asthma medication that would grant her relief and a greater lung capacity. Doctors had gauged her capacity at just 20 percent of normal when she had these attacks, and she had a bad one in Phoenix. "I didn't have the air to do it," Harding said, and she tried to smile. She probably shouldn't have smoked, either.

Michelle Kwan, just twelve years old, finished eighth. She was perky and inspiring, a classic pixie-in-waiting, in the mold of gymnasts Nadia Comeneci or Olga Korbut. A real charmer. Her day would come.

But after Kerrigan's.

Six

A Worldly Stumble

*The World Championships, March 1993,
Prague*

It had been thirty-two years since Prague
hosted the world championships of figure skating. Back then, both this golden city and the
U.S. figure-skating team were headed for terrible tragedies.

In 1961 Prague was starting to flex its politi-
cal independence from the former Soviet
Union, moving toward an encounter seven
years later with the Warsaw bloc tanks that the
Czechoslovaks had no chance of winning. The
U.S. skating team, which had earned gold med-

als in both the men's and women's competitions at the 1960 Olympics in Squaw Valley, met an even worse fate: the whole squad perished in an airplane crash on the way to the competition, the country's worst sporting disaster.

In 1993, fortunately, there was a sense of greater calm, even joy, in and around the aging Sports Hall. Prague, freed by the so-called Velvet Revolution instituted by President Václav Havel, was buzzing with tourists. The land of reform martyrs and Hapsburg castles was truly Bohemia again. Historic Charles Bridge pulsated with artists and with entrepreneurs who were a bit too busy to notice that a world-class athletic event was being hosted in their city. The stands would be half-empty all week, with tickets going for ridiculously low prices, even by the soft standards of Czech currency.

The U.S. team that arrived was fragile but promising. The men were marking time until Brian Boitano returned, but a young national champ, Scott Davis, was already the world's fastest spinner. Kerrigan was clearly the flagship skater among the women; she was the franchise. Ervin was too young, and Kwiatkowski was too limited, a token entry. Kerrigan was not at the top of her game, but most experts figured her nerves were strong enough to hold off the younger, less experienced Europeans and Asians. The experts were wrong.

Kerrigan was headed for her lowest moment as an amateur skater.

Her difficulties were evident already in practices at Prague. Physically she was healthy. On her landings she was fully capable of holding the outside or inside edge of her skating blade. But somehow she was not ready. She was over-rotating on some jumps. She was spending too much time picking herself up off the ice, brushing the chips off her fancy practice costumes. At an intense early practice at Prague, Witt sat rinkside and seemed to take some enjoyment at a tumble by Nancy Kerrigan of the United States, the twenty-three-year-old American champion. "She is always too nervous," Witt said critically.

Kerrigan rose just in time to watch a showy move by Oksana Baiul, the fifteen-year-old up-start from Ukraine. "She's got to do more than that," Kerrigan said to her coach, Evy Scotvold. Here was a fine demonstration of unfiltered, intergenerational jitters.

There were reasons for the nerves, reasons beyond the obvious stakes. For one thing, Kerrigan had dropped all consultations with a sports psychologist, against the wishes of her coaches. The use of a personal "head coach" is common among figure skaters, who must endure incredible pressure and maintain a razorlike concentration. The athletes are taught to confront their fears, sometimes to focus on a positive word or phrase during performances. But Kerrigan felt a personal psychologist would be too much of a stigma. She was trying to uphold her image as the perfect person, on and off the ice. The problem was, she wasn't perfect. Nobody is.

Kerrigan was also unaccustomed to this role of favorite on the world stage. She missed Kristi Yamaguchi, her friend, her confidante, and her legitimate alibi for finishing second. Kerrigan had comfortably deferred to Yamaguchi, whose talents she admired. Alone now, Kerrigan suddenly felt outnumbered by the huge international egos and curious celebrities who doubled as commentators.

Witt was in Prague as an analyst for NBC, to interview the skaters as they finished their routines. She was also on a scouting mission, because she planned a comeback of her own at the Lillehammer Olympics. "I am not going for the gold," said Witt, who was now twenty-seven years old and looking as formidable as ever. "But people want to hear different pop musicians, and they want to enjoy different kinds of actors and actresses. It is the same with skating. I can offer a different perform-ance, better for me than ever. And remember, the others must hit their triple jumps. They don't always do that, as we see."

Witt would be correct about Kerrigan's jitters, but not right away. America's great medal hope held up on the first day during the ladies' technical program, which would count for 33 percent of the final standing. Skating to "Paradise, the Master," by Mark Militano, Kerrigan was both solid and elegant. There was a triple lutz–double toe loop combination seventeen seconds into the program. Once she hit that, Kerrigan relaxed. She arched her back daintily for a layback spin, a position that hurt her back and one that she argued should not be a required technical move. "Sure, Nancy," Evy Scotvold would say, teasing her. "Anything you don't like, you shouldn't have to do."

Kerrigan nailed her double axel, wowed the audience with her grace on a circular step sequence, and finished with a spin combination that was a bit easier than it appeared. So simple. So stately. A standing ovation.

"It feels wonderful," Kerrigan said of her first-place perch. "I have more than just the jumps, and I think that makes a difference. But a lot of others here do, too. That's good to see."

Those closest to her crossed their fingers. Her coaches, Evy and Mary Scotvold, weren't so sure. Her parents also seemed to sense nothing was over quite yet. "If she can just hold it together for tomorrow, we'll be all set," said her father, Daniel. Nancy was dragged away from the media by her coaches, away from the attention and the pressure. Most of all, away from Oksana Baiul.

If she had bothered to peek over her shoulder, Kerrigan might have been petrified. There, skating a technical program directly after hers, was a fifteen-year-old athlete of formidable presence. This time Kerrigan did not turn around to watch Baiul of Ukraine. Talking straight into the television camera during her postprogram interview, she missed a great show, the indisputable birth of a star.

On the ice this day, Baiul was the most provocative of any skater. After Kerrigan's technical scores were posted—5.7's, 5.8's, and 5.9's, except for an obstinate British judge who gave her a 5.4—it was Baiul's turn to take the ice. But the fifteen-year-old teenager refused to start on cue. She continued to skate around center ice, demanding the attention of the audience before the music could begin.

"I listen to my skates," Baiul said of the blades purchased for her by fellow Ukrainian Viktor Petrenko. "They tell me when to start."

When she finally began, Baiul vamped her way through a surprisingly mature, flirtatious routine, filled with odd twists, spins, and grinds. There were no difficult combinations, but nobody seemed to notice this flaw. The judges were charmed by the sport's latest pixie.

"If she's like this at fifteen, imagine what she'll be like in a few years," said Michael Rosenberg, Baiul's agent. "I'm not even sure I want to know."

Kerrigan was not only facing Baiul, she was facing a growing legend, a heartbreaking story. Baiul's natural parents had died. She was an orphan, raised by her grandmother in Dnepropetrovsk, and her coach, Galina Zmievskaya. Her first coach, Stanislav Koretek, decided to emigrate to Canada, but before he left he delivered Baiul five hundred kilometers from Dnepropetrovsk to Odessa, to the doorstep of coach Galina Zmievskaya.

"We have a very difficult time now in Ukraine," Baiul said. "Difficult to skate, and difficult to live."

Baiul's arrival was a starburst. She had finished second in the European championships two months earlier, then waited for this moment in Prague. All week long she had been a compelling sight in practices and interviews. How could Kerrigan compete with the fresh tale of an orphaned Ukraine girl and with the other skaters, besides?

Surya Bonaly of France, attired in a leopard-skin outfit, was her usual athletic marvel. Her choice of costume was in questionable taste, however, and did not thrill the judges. But Bonaly nailed her jumps easily and skated more smoothly than in the past. Josee Chouinard of Canada stayed close, in fourth, with a flawless triple lutz–double toe loop combination. Lu Chen of China nearly crashed into the boards on her combination but righted herself and took fifth place. The pressure was now all on Kerrigan, who carried the additional burden of the American flag. The U.S. men had flopped, literally and figuratively. The women were no better. Kwiatkowski had been eliminated in preliminary qualifications, a true embarrassment and a lesson to those U.S. judges in Phoenix who had chosen her ahead of Tonya Harding and Nicole Bobek. Ervin, the only other American woman left in the competition, fell on her first triple jump and was hopelessly mired in fourteenth place after her routine.

The long program the next day would count for two-thirds of the final standing, and Kerrigan's coaches insisted that the extra ninety seconds in the routine on Friday would offer more breathing space to their skater. Kerrigan planned a triple-triple jump combination. If it was successful, she would be very difficult to beat.

"If the others want to win it, they've got to do it in the long program," Evy Scotvold said. "We'll see tomorrow if they can do it for four minutes. That's where Nancy's strongest, and that's where the truth shows through."

Unfortunately, Scotvold's words would come back to haunt him and his skater. Kerrigan's ambitious long program on Friday was a complete and utter disaster, for almost its entire four minutes. According to the blueprint, she was to land six triples, charming the audience with her interpretation of "Beauty and the Beast" from both the Walt Disney sound track and a New York Pops version. The lasting image was to be one of athleticism and grace, of a true champion. Instead, only panic showed through.

Here was the program, in theory: A triple flip. A triple lutz. A walley-walley-triple salchow combination. A flying camel. A side spin. A straight-line step sequence. A spiral. A triple toe loop–double loop combination. A spread-eagle into a triple loop. A camel combination spin. Back spiral variations. A triple salchow. A double axel. A spiral. A flying camel into a back sit.

Kerrigan came nowhere near that when it was finally her turn. First, though, she paced nervously backstage. She heard the cheers from the rink and tried to ignore them. Baiul, ailing with a bad back but nerveless, completed five triple jumps to a medley of Broadway music. Baiul was a sight for all eyes again, from the start of her performance. As she had on Friday before her technical program, Baiul refused to take her spot at center ice until she was fully prepared. She skated about like Mark Messier before a big face-off. She was more decorous than, but just as agile as, in her vampy technical program. Only near the end did she tire a bit, resulting in scores ranging from 5.6 to 5.9.

Bonaly stood in second place. Her seven triples failed to overtake Baiul, even though her routine was technically superior. Lu Chen of China was third. The programs of these three were not as sophisticated, or as balanced, as Kerrigan's at her best. Kerrigan was that great compromise, between the gymnastics of Bonaly and the modern dance of Baiul. The judges had made sure there was just enough room at the top for Kerrigan, if she could nail her program. They were holding 5.8's and 5.9's for her.

Skating second to last, Kerrigan fumbled and her hand touched down on an initial triple flip. She singled the triple lutz and stumbled on a triple salchow. She was finished, and she knew it. She became a skating, grimacing zombie. She successfully completed only two clean triples, finishing ninth in the long program and fifth overall. Her scores were appropriately disastrous, ranging from 5.0 to 5.3 on technical merit.

In the "kiss and cry" area afterward, Kerrigan was a public wreck, scornful of herself and other skaters. She broke down. Her mind was reeling. She couldn't hold her mind's replay. She turned to Mary Scotvold, her choreographer. "Can I try it again?" she asked. Later, in a corridor an hour after her terrible performance, Kerrigan bravely faced the American press. She might have ducked out on them. Instead she faced the music, and it sounded nothing like "Beauty and the Beast."

"What happened?" was the obvious query.

"I guess I felt more pressure than I admitted," Kerrigan said. "I haven't had a practice that bad, but my knees just weren't working, I guess.

"I'm just so mad at myself," she said. "I was awful. Obviously I've hit a pretty big low. I went from poor to terrible to horrible."

Her coach, Evy Scotvold, said he hoped the disappointment would turn Kerrigan's career around. Already she had committed herself to returning to a sports psychologist. She also talked about a greater attention, and dedication, to the details of practice. The endorsement parade would have to stop, or at least slow down.

"She was leading the pack, she was the favorite, and this was something she had never done before," Scotvold said. "I think she'll be better for this. She's disgusted with herself."

An American figure-skating official, nearly as distraught as Kerrigan, wondered that night at the Sports Hall if Kerrigan would ever reach her potential. "She's not strong enough," the official said. "She's a good skater, a good person, but she is not strong enough in her head to be a champion."

By dropping out of medal contention, Kerrigan put some extra pressure on herself for the future. She lost one berth for the United States team at the 1994 Olympics in Lillehammer, Norway. The American women would have only two spots now, instead of their customary three. The competition for those two berths, to be determined at the next U.S. championships in Detroit, figured to be cutthroat. Nobody yet knew just how cutthroat it would be.

Kerrigan had dug herself a deep hole, too, on the international level. She had lost some status, maybe even her position as Olympic heir apparent to Yamaguchi. Baiul had gained celebrity and respect. Her tale was now folklore. Baiul cried when she mounted the medal stand. She was, after all, just fifteen, the youngest world champion since Sonja Henie in 1927. "I have seen *Sun Valley Serenade*," said

Baiul, who knew little else of her movie star predecessor.

Most of all, Baiul cried. She cried when her coach, Zmievskaya, calmly finished her cup of coffee backstage and then informed Baiul that she was the gold medalist. "I didn't know what else to do," Baiul said.

That went for Kerrigan, too, whose eyes brimmed with tears most of the night. The Olympic dream seemed farther away now than it had a week earlier. There was some serious program tinkering, and mind altering, to be done. She was about to become very busy.

Seven

"Why Me?"

U.S. National Championships, January 1994, Detroit

There was no sense of impending disaster for Nancy Kerrigan in Detroit, when the national championships began in frigid weather at downtown Joe Louis Arena. Quite the contrary. In the preceding six months, Kerrigan had remade herself. She appeared self-confident and fine-tuned. She had demonstrated a total commitment to her sport. At last she appeared ready to take her place at the top of the pyramid.

Kerrigan had been through a lot in 1993.

There had been the lows of the world championships in Prague and a humiliating second-place finish at a Pro-Am competition in Los Angeles in April. There, Kerrigan had finished behind Caryn Kadavy, a 1988 Olympian who had not skated amateur programs for five years. "There's nowhere for me to go but up," she said.

Her coaches had despaired as well. They were no longer certain Kerrigan would ever be ready. "She has a confidence problem," Evy Scotvold said. "If she doesn't get the picture now, she never will."

Kerrigan got the picture. She and her coaches worked hard at both the mental and physical facets of the sport. She enlisted the services of a Boston sports psychologist, Cindy Adams, who helped her understand herself considerably better. She increased her practice hours at the Colonial Figure Skating Club in Dennis on Cape Cod and put aside some of the personal appearances that had sabotaged her in Prague. She also broke off her engagement, putting social activities on hold.

"I spent too much time on planes and not enough on the ice," Kerrigan said. "No one knew how I'd react. I'm the type of person who likes to be busy. But it affected me more than I thought it would."

One could delineate Kerrigan's commitment

to skating very simply: Before Prague. After Prague. Before Prague, Kerrigan trained two hours a day, five days a week. She skipped some of those practices whenever Reebok or Campbell's called, begging for a West Coast appearance. After Prague, she practiced three hours a day, six days a week. She dropped four pounds to 111, a significant weight loss for a figure skater. The slimmer the skater, the quicker the rotations on spins and jumps. She put off the endorsement demands with the help of agent Jerry Solomon at ProServ.

The strategies worked. Kerrigan sported a new, positive attitude that was hard to miss. Before a winning performance at a Pro-Am competition in Philadelphia in December 1993, Kerrigan sat at a table with a small group of reporters and spoke openly about her past fears and failures. It was a first, a break-through interview session. Sportswriters there left with filled notebooks and a new concept: Nancy Kerrigan as a good quote.

"In some ways, what happened in Prague might have been the best thing for me," Kerrigan said. "I was very mad at myself. It made me fight harder. With all the work I've done, I feel I'm good enough to win. I know it. Last year I thought it, but I really wasn't sure."

Her coach, Evy Scotvold, told the *Philadelphia Daily News* that he had never seen Kerrigan this way. "She is totally focused. I don't have to push her to train. In the past, she never wanted to practice more than one or two programs a day. Now she does them all and wants to do them perfectly. We used to have knock-down, drag-out fights. She would not do a complete program."

There was a psychological breakthrough when Adams helped Kerrigan understand her reluctance to practice her entire long program. Kerrigan came running to Scotvold with the revelation. "All that time, I was afraid to try a perfect program because I was afraid I would find out that I couldn't do it," Kerrigan had Scotvold.

"It was a profound thing to hear," Scotvold said.

The payoff for this metamorphosis became apparent in November, at the top-level Piruetten competition in Hamar, Norway. There, in the same rink where Kerrigan would have to skate at the Olympics, she was nearly perfect in her long program and finished first against some of the best skaters in the world. She finally nailed all five triples, retaining enough of her grace to earn six 5.9's from judges on artistic impression marks. In less than a year Kerrigan had reclaimed the number one world ranking and appeared headed for the Olympics as the gold-medal favorite.

"I think I'm the favorite, too," Kerrigan said.

"But is that good?" a reporter asked.

"Sure, why not?" Kerrigan said.

Kerrigan came to Detroit early in the week, settled into her downtown hotel, and began practices for what was supposed to be a relatively simple task. She was going to win the U.S. National Championships, a mere precursor to the Olympics. It was supposed to be a fait accompli, like Phoenix the year before. There really was no American out there to challenge her. At age thirteen, Michelle Kwan was still too young. Elaine Zayak, making an admirable comeback at age twenty-eight, was too old. Nicole Bobek couldn't stay on her skates. Lisa Ervin and Tonia Kwiatkowski had made no advances since their unspectacular performances in Prague.

That left Tonya Harding. Harding had dropped the Gillooly from her name after a recent divorce but was still considered the same unpredictable skater. Even if Harding skated one of her better programs and Kerrigan stumbled, Harding was unlikely to win. Harding was just too rough-edged, on and off the ice. She could pull off a triple axel, the hardest of all jumps for the women, and still get hammered in the marks for artistic impression.

At a press conference before the competition,

Harding seemed at ease with herself, sort of. She said her horoscope was good for the week, as was her stamina. Her breathing capacity was up to 44 percent. Harding also said that she had successfully shaken off a recent death threat made against her, which was reported at the northwest sectionals in Portland. There had been some suspicions about that threat, which allowed Harding to advance to the nationals without skating her program in Portland. A local official sent a memo by e-mail to another official, stating that Harding's people seemed to know about the threat before it was actually delivered to them.

"There were also a couple of bombs at a shopping mall," Harding said in Detroit.

"A couple of smoke bombs," said Diane Rawlinson, her coach, correcting her.

In any case, it was clear that Harding's act was far from together. So Kerrigan felt relatively secure in her favorite role as she headed for Cobo Arena and a training session on Thursday, January 6, one day before she was scheduled to skate her short program in competition. Kerrigan practiced her technical program without any problems, in white skirt and lacy top. She skated at the same time as rival Kwan.

Kwan's coach, Frank Carroll, was watching both skaters from across the boards when one of the most unbelievable events in the history of American sport began to unfold.

"Somebody very strange-looking, in a black jacket, carrying a camera, nudged me and asked me who a skater was, and I said, 'Nancy Kerrigan,' " Carroll said. "I didn't think twice about it until I heard the screaming."

The screaming. The screaming that would change this sport forever. Carroll, one of the true gentlemen of the sport, might have unwittingly tipped off the attacker. Maybe not. Another figure-skating coach, Kathy Stuart, said she had spotted a man fitting the attacker's description sitting in the stands minutes earlier, videotaping Kerrigan's performance and sweating profusely. Carroll's suspect had carried a thirty-five-millimeter camera.

Events swirled with great speed and confusion. Kerrigan finished practice. She walked past a curtain ten feet from the ice surface and paused to speak with a reporter, Dana Scarton, from the *Pittsburgh Post-Gazette*. A six-foot man dressed in black jacket and cap appeared from nowhere. He swung what appeared to be a metal rod at Kerrigan's knee, then ran down the corridor. "He ran real fast, crouched real low, and hit her in the legs," Scarton said. "He didn't say anything."

The assailant came to a set of locked doors—this clearly wasn't planned too well. He banged against one door until the Plexiglas splintered and fell out. He made his escape.

Meanwhile, Kerrigan had screamed and fallen backward. Grabbing her knee, she remained on the ground. "Why me? Why now?" she cried, calling for her father. "It hurts so bad," she moaned. "It hurts so bad."

Kerrigan was lifted from the floor by her father, who carried her from the practice area to a car for transport. In her frantic state, she asked her dad how far Ontario was from Detroit. She remembered a couple of strange letters from a fan there.

A video crew from InterSport, in town to gether interviews for a special on Dorothy Hamill, caught the aftermath of the attack on tape. Kevin Cusick, a freelance producer working with the InterSport crew, chased after the unidentified attacker. A woman screamed, "Somebody stop him!"

The assailant ran past a group of auto show conventioneers from the Ford Motor Company who were boarding a bus outside the arena. The passengers screamed at Cusick, pointed in the direction of the attacker, and told Cusick to follow the man who had run off into the night. "I tried to get one of them to come with me, but none of them wanted to," Cusick said. The man vanished. That was as close as anybody would get to the assailant for the next few days.

Kerrigan was treated for a badly bruised knee at nearby Hutzel Hospital by orthopedic surgeon Steven Plomaritis, then released. She walked without assistance, but with a limp. She spent the night recovering in her hotel room after canceling a practice session.

"It's a serious bruise, a direct blow to the kneecap," Plomaritis said. "It may preclude her from participating."

This was now the ultimate nightmare, for Kerrigan, for the figure-skating world, for Detroit, for America, for the sports world. Like the attack on Monica Seles ten months earlier in Hamburg, this assault underscored the vulnerability of top female athletes. If Kerrigan did not skate her short program the next day, U.S. Figure Skating Association officials initially said, she would not qualify for the Olympics. Rules were rules. "I don't think we can change the rules here," said Paul George, the Olympic representative for the USSF. "Maybe for the next one. You learn from experience. But there are mechanisms that we would have to go through."

It appeared that Kerrigan might never live out her Olympic dream.

Dr. Plomaritis said that pain, not permanent disability, would determine whether Kerrigan could compete. Her agent, Jerry Solomon from

ProServ, said he hoped that Kerrigan could continue.

"She's a tough competitor, and she doesn't like what happened to her," Solomon said. "But she has to get over the emotional side of this. Nancy is determined, but she is scared. She's also aware of the rules. She's very concerned about being within the rules."

Immediately, security questions were raised by Kerrigan's coaches and friends. A local firm, Crowd Management, was placed in charge of security at Cobo Arena. "This was an area where security was provided by the ice-skating people," said Cliff Russell, press secretary for Detroit's new mayor, Dennis Archer. "Police officers were not allowed in this area." This sounded like a feeble alibi to many skaters and coaches, who had never before heard of police being ordered out of any place by anyone. Detroit, already suffering through blizzard conditions and a loss of heat and hot water in the downtown area, suffered another black eye.

"There was no security," complained Evy Scotvold, who was near where the attack took place. "We're just happy the guy didn't go for her head. It's a terrible thing, but that's the world we live in." Witnesses reported that nobody was checking credentials in the practice area at Cobo Arena and that the suspect might have forged his own anyway. At adjacent Joe Louis Arena, where Kerrigan and the other skaters performed their competitive programs, a guard was napping at his post minutes before the Kerrigan incident.

Atanas Ilitch, vice president of Olympic Arenas, insisted that security was "high through day one."

"This appears to be a premeditated incident," Ilitch said.

Detroit police detective Vito Vario said his department was uncertain of the motive for the attack on Kerrigan. Solomon, her agent, could not say, either. "She gets a lot of letters saying a lot of things. But nothing to put us in a frame of mind to be fearful."

The police investigation, joined soon by the FBI, branched out in three different directions: Portland, Texas, and Ontario. One police source said the department had received suspicious phone calls after the incident from Portland and Texas. Harding's fan club also was headquartered in Portland. Two eyewitnesses had looked at the attacker squarely in the face. But as of yet police were uncertain whether the assailant was white or black. There would be two composite sketches, and neither was going to help very much.

U.S. Figure Skating Association officials huddled into the night. Everybody was fairly certain by now that Kerrigan would have to withdraw, that she could not heal in time. They were trying to figure out if there was a way to put her on the team anyway. By now it was evident that the organization would be crucified by the public, and by the U.S. Olympic Committee, if it excluded Kerrigan. After all, she had been a certain Olympian. She had been attacked on the USFSA's watch.

Finally, after scouring the international competition rulebook, they came across rule No. 5.05 (page 193), which stated that the USSF could consider "other competitors who did not compete" in the nationals. Claire Ferguson, president of the USFSA, began circulating the news among Kerrigan's coaches and among reporters: There might be a way out of this, thanks to rule 5.05. "Read the rule, and we'll have a statement in the morning," Ferguson said. The U.S. Olympic Committee, anxious to do the right thing, said it would consider any requests to consider a qualifying exception in this case.

Dr. LeRoy Walker, president of the USOC, promised that his organization would look into better security for athletes at its next meeting. Harvey Schiller, executive director of the United States Olympic Committee, turned up the heat on the USFSA to do something for Kerrigan. "She has been the victim of a sense-

Preparing to begin her routine at the Oakland competition, Nancy is a portrait of concentration and beauty. *(Shirley McLaughlin)*

Above: Picture Perfect. *(Joe Brown) Right:* Spinning dreams of gold. Nancy at the 1992 World Championships in Oakland. *(Shirley McLaughlin)*

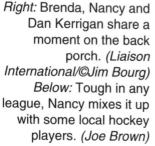

Right: Brenda, Nancy and Dan Kerrigan share a moment on the back porch. *(Liaison International/©Jim Bourg)*
Below: Tough in any league, Nancy mixes it up with some local hockey players. *(Joe Brown)*

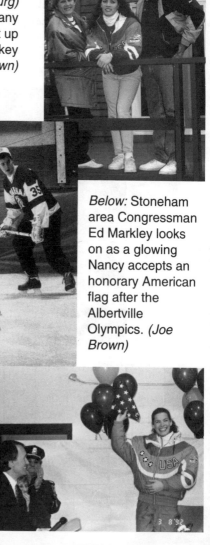

Below: Stoneham area Congressman Ed Markley looks on as a glowing Nancy accepts an honorary American flag after the Albertville Olympics. *(Joe Brown)*

Nancy's father, Dan Kerrigan, bursts with pride as he watches the parade in Nancy's honor. March 8, 1992.
(Joe Brown)

Hours of practice separate the good from the great. Nancy polishes her routine for the 1990 Goodwill Games in Tacoma, Washington.
(Shirley McLaughlin)

YEA NANCY says it all. Stoneham, Massachusetts prepares for the Nancy Kerrigan Day Parade, March 8, 1992. *(Joe Brown)*

The town of Stoneham decks the town hall for the celebration of Nancy Kerrigan Day. March 8, 1992. *(Joe Brown)*

Above: Nancy speaks to the press prior to the AT&T U.S. Pro Am. December 1993. *(Shirley McLaughlin)*
Left: Local girl makes good. Nancy takes a victory ride through downtown Stoneham. *(Joe Brown)*

Left: Tonya Harding completes her singles routine in the 1987 U.S. Nationals. *(©1994 Paul Harvath)*
Below: Concerned coach Evy Stotvold (left) and Dr. Mahlon Bradley (right) look on as Nancy speaks to the press about the assault in Detroit. January 10, 1993. *(Joe Brown)*

Knowing her time is coming, bronze medalist Nancy watches as Tonya Harding accepts the Gold Medal in the 1991 U. S. Nationals. Kristi Yamaguchi won the silver. *(Shirley McLaughlin)*

Above Left: Nancy's focus and intensity are mirrored in the faces of the spectators during the 1991 U.S. Nationals. *(Shirley McLaughlin) Above:* Nancy and partner Paul Wylie glide effortlessly through a perfect turn during the 1992 World Tour. *(Shirley McLaughlin) Left:* Executing a flawless landing at the U.S. Pro Am in December 1993. *(Shirley McLaughlin)*

Taking a well-deserved bow with partner Paul Wylie during the 1992 World Tour Show. *(Shirley McLaughlin)*

Above: America's Sweetheart "rocks out" in Tacoma during the 1993 World Tour. *(Shirley McLaughlin)*
Right: A pensive moment during the AT&T U. S. Pro Am in Philadelphia. December 1993. *(Shirley McLaughlin)*

less and brutal act, but she has demonstrated toughness and the competitive spirit that only an Olympian would have," Schiller said in a press statement. "We wish Nancy Kerrigan the best of luck in her dream of making this 1994 Olympic team."

In fact, Kerrigan was just trying to sort things out, like any other victim after a shocking assault. She appeared briefly on "ABC Sports" that night. "It's just one bad guy," she told "ABC Sports." "Not everybody's like that." Then she tried to sleep. She would wake up in the morning and see if she could skate. "I am going to see how I practice and jump," she said. But the assailant had known what he was doing. He had hit her on the right leg, her landing leg. It would take a miracle for her to skate so quickly.

Kerrigan gave up on her practice after the swelling went behind the knee and a doctor told her she would have to rest the joint. She was shattered. She had spent her whole life trying to get to the top of the medal stand at Lillehammer. Her future earnings and her historical place in the sport were now in the hands of the bureaucrats—not out on the ice, where they belonged.

Kerrigan appeared the next day at the Joe Louis rink, along with family, friends, and doctors. Dr. Mahlon Bradley, an orthopedic surgeon for the USFSA, broke the news that Kerrigan could not skate, that she was out of the U.S. National Championships. She had been lucky that her assailant had not struck her an inch lower, directly on the knee. Her career might have ended right there. "The decision not to skate was made by the medical staff based on pain, lack of motion, and lack of strength in the knee," Bradley said. "She is unable to do what she needs to compete. Even after local anesthesia, there was a lack of motion and she was unable to control a hopping motion."

Twenty cubic centiliters of blood had been drained from the knee. A magnetic resonance image test would be performed in a few days. But Bradley said he was hopeful Kerrigan could skate at the Olympics, if the USFSA added her to the team.

Kerrigan came later to meet the press. Her hair was down now, tousled. She wrung her hands. She fought through tears to say she was angry and frightened about the attack. Her voice cracked with emotion during a twenty-five-minute press conference. She was holding it together, an impressive performance worthy of the highest marks.

"I've never worked so hard as this year," Kerringan said. "I'm pretty upset and angry. I wanted to skate. I just wanted to show everybody I didn't lose it.

"It's hard to say how long I'll look over my shoulder to see who's behind me," she went on. "I hope they catch him, so he can never do this to anybody else again. I shouldn't have said, 'Why me?' I should have said, 'Why anybody?'"

"I didn't get a lot of sleep last night," she concluded. "I don't know what I was dreaming, but I was twitching. Nerves, I think." She was then asked about her chances for the Olympics. "I'm not sure about the rules," Kerrigan said. "My job is to skate. I'll do whatever I have to do to get ready if chosen."

Kerrigan's father and mother sat next to her. Both were shaken at least as much as their daughter. "I am angry, and it is unbelievable that this could happen," said Brenda Kerrigan. "Everybody loves Nancy."

A reporter asked Brenda Kerrigan if she ever thought that a competitor's fan might have done this. Already rumors were flying about Harding's rabid fan club. "I have thought about it, but I don't even want to talk about it," said her mother.

Dan Kerrigan had talked and talked with his daughter. Together they could still not figure this thing out. "She's heartbroken," he said. "Nancy cannot understand why someone would do this."

Evy Scotvold was her loudest, strongest advocate on the Olympic front. "Nancy is the number one–ranked skater in this country based on international competitions over the last several months," he said. "We cannot let a vicious criminal prevent her from the team if she is able to go."

Nancy Kerrigan watched the women skate their short programs on Friday, from high above the arena in a luxury box. She watched the long program on Saturday from there, too, signing autographs for young fans and waiting to hear whether she would be added to the team after the competition was over.

Harding won. She did not try her triple axel, but she skated almost flawlessly. "This is only half a title," she said, coughing through an asthma attack. "It won't be a complete title without competing against Nancy."

Harding was even more emotional than usual. "I am the Tonya Harding everyone really believes in," she said. "I know who my true friends are. I'm on my way." Then Harding thanked New York Yankee owner George Steinbrenner for his financial support. (He had given her $20,000 toward her annual $50,000 in training bills.) Later, to the consternation of the figure-skating world, Harding said that when she faced Kerrigan in the Olympics, she would "whip her butt."

"I don't see anybody as my top competition," Harding said. "I'm the only one I have to beat. You guys [the media] say I'm controversial, so maybe I am. I'm kind of like the Charles Barkley of figure skating. A lot of people like me being open-minded and doing what I think is right. Some don't. That's who I am."

When the competition was done, the USFSA's forty-five-member international committee required just eight minutes to vote unanimously to add Kerrigan to the Olympic team. She would bump Michelle Kwan, the thirteen-year-old. Kwan was gracious about it. So was Carroll, Kwan's coach. "Nancy deserves to go," Carroll said. "She would have won here, I honestly believe that. It was not her fault that she didn't win."

It was while submitting to a mandatory drug test that Kerrigan found out she would be a member of the team—hardly a romantic setting. She returned to her box and raised her arms in triumph. "I'm feeling better already," she said. "I'll be ready."

The next day, on Sunday, Kerrigan appeared even healthier. Again, without a limp, she made her way onto the ice for a photograph with her Olympic teammates. She was placed next to Harding, in the front row. Kerrigan sat straight and smiled, looking like a million dollars in her sequined white dress. Harding appeared almost dowdy in her garish purple outfit with the plunging see-through neckline. She was a well-conditioned athlete, with great upper-body strength. But when she sat, she slumped, and her bare arms appeared deceptively flabby. These two were a study in contrasts and in packaging. It was a photo that would be used in newspapers and magazines again and again, in the days to come.

Nobody knew that yet.

Eight

The Investigation

When the championships concluded in Detroit, it looked as if the Nancy Kerrigan case would never be solved. There were too many leads in this felonious assault, too many phone calls from would-be Samaritans, and not enough hard evidence.

Investigators had begun their probe with two letters that Kerrigan received from an obsessive fan somewhere in Ontario. These were the letters that had come into Kerrigan's mind immediately after she was attacked, while in the arms of her father. Since the Ontario province was just across the Detroit River from

Cobo Arena, Kerrigan was quickly persuaded to hand over the letters to police.

The first was a love letter that Kerrigan said was "nothing bad." The second letter was angrier, complaining that Kerrigan had not responded to the first. Both were obsessive and troubling in their vivid, exaggerated description of the skater. "They were about me and my figure," Kerrigan said, looking uncomfortable discussing the matter. "They were nice, but they were kind of strange. That's why I didn't answer them."

Detroit deputy police chief Benny Napoleon would not comment on the letters, but Kerrigan confirmed they had a return address and could be easily traced. This became a quick dead end. The fan was just a fan. After a visit from police, he probably would never write another letter to anybody.

Shortly after midnight on Friday morning, only hours after Kerrigan was attacked, police handcuffed a spectator who was watching the top women practice at Joe Louis Arena. He had been seen earlier in the day, trying to gain access to the dressing area. There would be no security lapses anymore, no chances taken. After some questioning, police were convinced that the man was merely a disorderly fan, and he was released. "He is not a suspect," Napoleon said.

Napoleon, a genial man with an instinctive way around the media, would normally busy himself with murders and manslaughters, not with bashed kneecaps. But the police chief said he believed that this felonious assault deserved his special attention. "You're talking about a world-class figure skater," Napoleon said. "This is not just a person hit on the knee. It's like the difference between my old horse breaking his leg and Ruffian breaking her leg."

Two eyewitnesses had seen the attacker flee, but the composite sketches drawn from interviews were too vague to do much good. Three days after the attack, police were still changing the description of the suspect from white to black and back again. There was also the videotape shot by the InterSport crew. Through special enhancement techniques, police were able to isolate and spotlight the shadow of the attacker in one frame. Napoleon sounded hopeful. He said that enhancement might yet identify the man. "We have the face," he said. "We have the eyes, the nose, the mouth." In truth, however, this was a bit of a technological bluff. The assailant had been nothing but a tiny blur in the original videotape. The resulting photos, after enhancement, were fuzzy at best. Napoleon said that the tape would be enhanced some more, but nobody was kidding himself in Detroit. Enhancement had its limits. Videotape technology was not going to nab the criminal.

Far more promising were ongoing probes in Portland, land of Tonya Harding and her loyal supporters. Police detectives and the FBI were investigating several leads, because a couple of suspicious postattack phone calls had been made from the area. The working hypothesis—a bit off the mark, as it turned out—was that the attack on Kerrigan had been carried out either by a Harding fan or by a hitman hired by a Harding fan.

The Tonya Harding Fan Club had nearly five hundred devoted members in and around the Portland area. There was also a newsletter, *The Skater*, edited by Joe Haran, which at times targeted Kerrigan for criticism. The newsletter regularly complained that Kerrigan was the darling of skating judges; that she was assured of first place in competitions, regardless of how she skated. In the past, Haran had some run-ins with journalists whom he believed had written negative articles about Harding. The *Oregonian*, the daily paper in Portland, once reported to police that Haran had made a disturbing phone call to one of its columnists. After the assault on Kerrigan, Haran called an editor at the *Oregonian* and said, "I bet you think I did this, don't you?" Haran had nothing to do with the assault, but Detroit police wanted to make certain. They interviewed Julie Vader, the *Oregonian* columnist, about Haran's calls.

The U.S. National Championships ended on Sunday, with an exhibition by the top skaters that would be taped and telecast at a later time. The nation's media packed its bags and headed out, fully believing that the Kerrigan investigation would drag on for months with little to show for it. Kerrigan's plea "Why me?" sounded like a riddle for the ages. Even Kerrigan realized there might be no explanation forthcoming. "This sort of crime happens to people all the time," she said. "I just happen to be famous."

But by the next day, on Monday, events had begun to percolate in Portland. A bulbous-looking man named Shawn Eckardt, Harding's bodyguard, had started the ball rolling. Eckardt, a bit of a blowhard and a self-proclaimed antiterrorist expert, weighed 350 pounds and liked to drive around town, very publicly, in his 1976 green four-door Mercury. Eckardt brought a tape recording to a friend, a local minister named Eugene C. Saunders, and played it. The tape, recorded surreptitiously during a phone call, documented a three-way discussion. Eckardt told Saunders that one voice was his own, and another belonged to Jeff Gillooly, Harding's ex-husband. The third,

Eckardt said, was an acquaintance from Phoenix, who was being asked to perform a hit of some kind on Kerrigan for a sum of money. The words were chilling, suggesting that Kerrigan had been fortunate to survive the attack.

"Why don't we just kill her?" asked one voice, identified as Gillooly's.

"We don't need to kill her. Let's just hit her in the knee," Eckardt reportedly responded on the tape.

Eckardt asked Saunders what to do with this information. Saunders did not know, either. He went to a mutual friend, Gary Crowe. Crowe, thirty, was a Portland private investigator with thirteen years' experience. He listened to Saunders, his trusted friend, as Saunders discussed the contents of the taped conversation. "Gene only told me about those two lines from the tape," Crowe said. "They were so memorable, he could repeat them."

Crowe advised Saunders to go to the district attorney's office, and according to Crowe, that is what Saunders did. On Monday, Saunders talked to the DA. On Tuesday, he talked to the FBI.

By Tuesday night, Crowe could no longer contain himself. He could not keep his secret. He went public with his blockbuster thirdhand information. He was inundated by interviewers from network news and tabloid TV shows, all of whom lined up in the corridors outside his office. He said he believed whatever Saunders told him: "He's a straight shooter, the straightest of the straight." He warned, however, that he could not vouch for the trustworthiness of Eckardt.

"I believe every single word that Mr. Saunders said," Crowe said. "He heard those things on the tape. I don't know that the things on the tape were true. Mr. Eckardt likes to be the center of attention sometimes." In fact, Eckardt had flunked out of bodyguard school in Phoenix and boasted a résumé filled with misstatements and misspellings.

Crowe told the world that the Kerrigan-bashing plot had evolved this way: Gillooly approached Eckardt and asked Eckardt to set up the hit. Eckardt then called an associate in Arizona, the hitman. Crowe's theory was that the hitman had not been paid and that Eckardt went public because he feared retribution. Crowe said he did not think Harding was directly involved.

In fact, the alleged conspiracy was far more complex than this and involved at least one other person. Much misinformation was printed over the next few days by the national media, which tried its best but could hardly keep up with the pace of these stunning developments. Everybody got the general idea: Authorities believed there was a conspiracy to attack Kerrigan, and Harding's bodyguard and ex-husband were involved. The story, already enormous, became a national obsession. Arraignments would be carried live on CNN, like some prime-time miniseries. Eventually the story made the front covers of *The New York Daily News, Newsday, Sports Illustrated, The New York Times*, and scores of other publications.

Before he was ordered to shut up by his attorney, Gillooly told the *Oregonian* in Portland that he was innocent of any involvement. "I wouldn't do that," he said. "I have more faith in my wife than to bump off the competition."

Harding spoke with the FBI twice in that first week and for a ten-hour session with investigators the next week. She continued to maintain her complete innocence. She canceled a skating exhibition appearance in Fairfax, Virginia, but began practicing again at her rink in Portland. "I've talked to the FBI and given them all the information I have," Harding said. "I worked my butt off for this, and if anybody wanted to beat Nancy, it was me. Who wanted to compete against her the most? It was me."

Investigators did not believe Gillooly. They relied on the information from Eckardt, who confessed to the plot. Eckardt said he felt tremendous remorse about his role the instant he saw Kerrigan suffering on national television. On the morning of January 11, Eckardt allegedly purchased a $20 Fone America card to make two calls from pay phones in northeast Portland to the house of a Derrick Smith in Arizona. Two more calls were made from pay phones that afternoon. Supposedly, the calls were made to corroborate stories.

Eckardt was arrested on January 13. Working on tips from Eckardt, Portland investigators soon issued arrest warrants for Shane Stant, the alleged hitman who would turn himself in; Derrick Smith, Stant's uncle and accused middle man in the plot; and, soon, Gillooly. The alleged weapon, a collapsible metal baton, was recovered from a dustbin outside the Cobo Hall arena. Less than two weeks after the assault, all four men were arraigned and faced either conspiracy or assault charges. If convicted on the conspiracy charge, Gillooly was unlikely to spend more than two years in prison. Although he had a volatile history with Harding, he had no previous criminal record.

When federal law enforcement officials in Portland released affidavits in the case, the bizarre plot was outlined in detail for everybody to read. It was, the authorities claimed, a clear-cut case of getting Kerrigan out of the way so that Harding could win the title. It was also a botched, clumsy effort by thugs who seemed incapable of showing up at the right rink at the right time.

The attack went this way, according to the information gathered by investigators: Stant and Smith drove from their homes near Phoenix to Portland on December 26 for a meeting with Eckardt at the bodyguard's home. Acting as agent for Gillooly, Eckardt asked Stant and Smith to injure Kerrigan. In exchange, he offered the men future jobs as bodyguards for Harding that would pay them $1,000 per week apiece—a relatively paltry sum for such dirty, dangerous work. But then, these men could hardly be considered professional hitmen.

According to law enforcement officials, Stant and Smith agreed to the deal. Gillooly gave Eckardt $2,000 in hundred-dollar bills, which Eckardt then gave to Smith. Smith gave the money to Stant for travel expenses. Much of the money allegedly used to carry out the conspiracy was later traced to Harding's Memorial Fund, a pool from public and private contributors set aside for amateur skaters by the U.S. Figure Skating Association. It was to this fund that Steinbrenner had donated $20,000. Steinbrenner also donated useful funds to such skaters as Nicole Bobek, Michelle Kwan, and junior skater Amanda Ward. In theory, Gillooly might have had access to the money in the fund without Harding's knowledge.

Stant began stalking Kerrigan in Boston and Cape Cod, where she practiced in the town of South Dennis, more than a week before the attack in Detroit. He never bothered to use an alias during this entire time. Stant flew to Boston from Portland on December 28. He stayed for two nights near Boston Harbor, at the Logan Airport Hilton, before he headed to Cape Cod and checked into the Gull Wing Suites motel on Route 28. Oregon authorities said there were three calls on December 28 to the Tony Kent arena from the home in Oregon City shared by Gillooly and Harding. Eckardt claimed that Gillooly told him these calls came from Harding, who was trying to find out Kerrigan's practice times. Later, according to Eckardt, Gillooly told him that Harding was so concerned about the appearance of these calls, she was already preparing an alibi for them in case she was questioned. She was going to say that she intended to ask Kerrigan to autograph posters for Harding's fans.

Stant went to the rink on New Year's Eve, but Kerrigan was gone. She was with her parents for the holiday in Stoneham, a few miles north of Boston. Stant stayed on the Cape, in the motel. *The New York Times* reported that Stant spent $90 a night on his room, quickly eating into his expense money. A phone call was made from Stant's room to the rink again on January 1.

On January 3, after another call from the Gillooly-Harding home to the arena, Kerrigan arrived at Tony Kent. "She was only here for a short time," Dottie Larkin, the manager of the rink, told *The New York Times.* "The weather was getting bad, we had some light snow, and the parking lot had ice on it. She had a costume fitting in New York and then had to fly to Detroit." Larkin said nobody had spotted the two-hundred-pound Stant in the rink while Kerrigan was there or at any other time. "He would kind of stand out in a crowd," she said.

Kerrigan headed to New York for promotional work before going to the U.S. National Championships. Stant bought a $125 ticket on a Greyhound Bus from Boston to Detroit, to ambush Kerrigan there. On January 4, he checked into the Super 8 Motel at Romulus, Michigan, near the airport. His room, with a water bed, cost $33.92 per night. From this hotel, Stant reportedly made several calls to Oregon and Arizona. Stant rented a brown General Motors car from Alamo, near his motel. Meanwhile, also on January 4 in Portland, Eckardt independently asked a casual acquaintance, Russell Reitz, whether he was interested in killing somebody for $65,000. Reitz looked at Eckardt as though he were crazy and declined. Eckardt then asked Reitz if he would consider breaking somebody's legs for the same amount. Again, the answer was no.

"I've got a hit in Detroit. I'll just have to send my team," Eckardt said, according to Reitz, who dismissed this boast as the rantings of a braggart.

On January 5, the day before the attack, authorities say Stant cased Cobo Arena. He might have been out of money by then, because Eckardt wired another $750 to Smith. Smith met Stant later at the Detroit airport. The two reportedly split a pizza and the money.

In an interview Eckardt gave to the *Oregonian*, the bodyguard claimed that Harding had become impatient with the men who were supposed to be plotting against Kerrigan. She wanted to know what was taking so long. "You know, you need to stop screwing around with this and get it done," Harding said, according to Eckardt. Also according to Eckardt, Gillooly offered Stant and Smith a $10,000 bonus, directly from the U.S. Figure Skating Association Memorial Fund, if the attack on Kerrigan was carried out quickly. George Steinbrenner, chief contributor, would have loved to hear that one.

On January 6, when the attack took place, Stant and Smith went to Cobo Arena to case the place again. Smith was to be the getaway man, according to authorities. After the attack and escape, Smith phoned Eckardt and received another $1,300 in Detroit. According to reports, the hitmen had discussed the possibility of blackmailing Gillooly. There never was time. Back in Portland, Eckardt reportedly bragged of the hit to Reitz the same night it happened.

The Kerrigans, for the most part, tried to stay as far as possible from the ongoing investigations. That was important for Nancy's mind-set. But the family wanted to be certain that the probe would proceed as smoothly and thoroughly as possible. Brenda Kerrigan contacted Senator Ted Kennedy on January 13, asking him to make certain that the investigation remained at the federal level and was not turned over exclusively to local authorities in Detroit and Portland. Kennedy became an active lobbyist on behalf of the Kerrigans, passing along the family's concern to the Justice Department. The FBI stayed on the case. About fifteen FBI agents stationed in Portland worked on the case, in conjunction with local authorities in Portland and Detroit. A grand jury extended its deliberations into February, as the world waited for indictments to be handed down.

When Kerrigan flew to Los Angeles on January 22 to tape a Reebok commercial, she took advantage of an Oregon state law that allows victims to obtain information about developments in the probe. Portland investigators and two FBI agents flew to Los Angeles to confer with Kerrigan. The intrigue was irresistible, even for Kerrigan.

"It's a great story and would be fun to watch on television if it were someone else," Jerry Solomon, Kerrigan's agent, told *Newsweek*. "But it's her, so it's bizarre."

While all this was going on, the U.S. Figure Skating Association grappled with its own dilemma: what to do with Harding. It would not be an easy decision. If the USFSA kicked Harding off the team, it could be accused of presuming guilt too quickly on the skater's part. If it kept her on the team, it was faced with a monumental logistical and public relations problem at Lillehammer.

Arrangements were made in Lillehammer to obtain lodging for first alternate Michelle Kwan, just in case. Second alternate Nicole Bobek was also told to keep practicing. Nationwide, columnists and public opinion polls tried to push the USFSA one way, then another. One telephone poll in the *New York Daily News* found that more than 90 percent of its respondents wanted Harding off the team.

"We won't be bullied by columnists or public opinion polls," said one U.S. Olympic Committee official. "We've got to make a reasonable decision."

Somehow, reason didn't seem to have very much to do with this case.

Nine

Tale of Two Skaters

If the attack on Kerrigan was supposed to sabotage her career, it had certainly failed. Kerrigan was more popular now than ever, an international symbol of survival in an insane, violent world. Within four days of the assault, Kerrigan's knee regained 75 percent of its full motion. Within two weeks she was completing her most difficult jumps in practice: the double axel and triple lutz. She was going to be fine. Her Olympic dreams were alive. Her earnings potential skyrocketed.

"Nancy's picture has been all over the world," said Michael Rosenberg, the agent for world-champion Oksana Baiul. "If anything, she's more marketable than ever."

A medal of any kind in Lillehammer would earn her millions of dollars. A gold medal would be worth $25 million or more, if touring money and endorsements were included in the total. A skater of Kerrigan's stature, adorned with a gold medal, might pull in $3 million per year from the Tom Collins skating tour, at least until the next queen was crowned at the 1998 Olympics.

The money, of course, was only part of it. Just getting back on the ice near her home in Stoneham and performing her jumps had been the real triumph for Kerrigan. Slowly, over the course of a few frigid days in mid-January, she tested her right leg with step sequences, then with spins, and finally with jumps. There was nothing to hide. Journalists were invited to watch and film many of her practices and to talk to Kerrigan during postworkout press conferences.

She had been fortunate in at least two respects. The competition schedule had been helpful, with an unusually early national championship and an unusually late Olympics. This gave her a full six weeks to recover. Also, the nasty chop to her leg had struck relatively pliant muscles, not bone or ligament. There was no tear, no break. On January 15, her first day back on the ice, Kerrigan was carefully monitored by Dr. Mahlon Bradley, the orthopedic surgeon who had worked with her since the incident. She performed only basic steps. "My knee was a little stiff, and it took some time to get loosened up," she said. "But it felt good to be on the ice again."

By the next day, Kerrigan was more limber. She said she couldn't wait to start jumping. "It's a little boring without the jumps," she said. "If I had to skate my Olympic program today, I think I could."

Every day was better. The well-wishes continued to pour in from all over. Autograph seekers lined up outside the rink. Stacks of fan mail were piled on the hall table of her Stoneham home, waiting for her whenever she found a break in her practice schedule. It seemed as though half the politicians in America had called. Ditto for celebrities. There were the flowers from Adam Oates, the letter from Mark Messier.

Kerrigan's psychological recovery, however, was not complete. She was a battler, but the memory of that afternoon ambush in Detroit lodged stubbornly in her subconscious. "I was at a party, and I was watching a little kid," Kerrigan told *People* magazine, yet another publication that featured her on its cover. "Suddenly I turned around, and there was someone standing with a bag of potato chips in their hand, which was close to my head when I turned. It scared me for a second—and I jumped."

Paul Wylie, the former Olympic silver medalist and a training partner, reported that Kerrigan was still "confused" by events, but that she was not obsessed by the attack. It helped that Kerrigan had her support system in place. Her coaches, the Scotvolds, were there. Her family was there, in the doctors' offices. Brenda Kerrigan pressed her face against a screen so that she could examine a magnetic resonance image of her daughter's right knee. The mother remembered a time when she'd told a young Nancy to suffer in silence, when her skates were too small and there was no money yet to buy a larger size. Nancy did as she was told.

"I know my daughter," Brenda Kerrigan said. "I don't believe she needs any help to get over this. She's tough. She's strong."

The Kerrigans and her close friends were there for Nancy, just in case. Three thousand miles away, in Portland, Oregon, Tonya Harding had no such luxury. Her parents visited her briefly at the rink, then left. Harding no longer could be certain about anybody. Too many of her acquaintances, her former protectors, were lining up to turn state's evidence against her. Harding, like Kerrigan, had grown up in a working-class background. Unlike Kerrigan, she'd never received strong emotional support from her family. Her father, Al, a laborer, left Portland in 1987 after divorcing her mother, LaVona, a waitress who had married six times. For most of a year the family had lived in a trailer. LaVona and Tonya would collect recyclable cans and bottles along the roadside in order to fund the skater's training, and the mother often sewed Tonya's costumes herself. LaVona's relationship with her daughter was volatile. Tonya liked her father better, but he was not often around.

Before he left, Al Harding taught his daughter some skills not normally associated with figure-skating queens. Harding learned to shoot a cut-down .22 at the age five. She learned to repair cars and split wood. She worked hard at her skating, like Kerrigan. Harding had a great natural athleticism. She loved the freedom that skating represented. Then, at the age of fifteen, she met Jeff Gillooly.

From the start, the pairing seemed ill fated, a potent mixture of flame and fury. While preparing for her first real date with Gillooly, Harding was involved in a violent confrontation with a half brother. When the incident was reported to police, Harding received only ambiguous support from her family. It drove

another emotional wedge between her and her
parents.

Harding and Gillooly were married in March
1990, but theirs was never a simple springtime
romance. At the wedding reception, her father,
Al, reportedly told the groom, "I never liked
you, but welcome to the family." After that,
the pair's stormy relationship kept the figure-
skating community aghast and gabbing in the
arena corridors. The couple was separated at
least twice, amid rumors of infidelity, gunplay,
and possible abuse. When Tonya Harding filed
for divorce in a Portland court for the first time
in June 1991, she complained that Gillooly
"wrenched my arm and wrist and pulled my
hair and shoved me."

"I'm scared for my safety," she testified, and
obtained a restraining order against her husband to keep him away. Her mother, LaVona,
told *Sports Illustrated* in 1992, "I knew Jeff
had a violent streak. Once, he tried to break
down the door."

The couple was reunited in 1992, then separated again in 1993, heading toward a divorce
in August. Again, Harding sought protection
from a judge. "He told me to watch my back.
He follows me and has broken into my house
and into my truck, and I am afraid for my
safety," she wrote about Gillooly. The *Oregonian* reported that Harding suspected Gillooly

of stealing her truck during this separation period. According to the paper, Harding approached two men at an east-side gym where she worked out in Portland and told them that she wanted Gillooly "taken care of."

"She said that most people wanted $100,000 for this kind of job because of who she was," reported the *Oregonian*. "They laughed it off, but they had no doubt she was serious." Days later, the paper reported, Harding changed the offer and asked if anybody would be willing simply to beat up Gillooly.

The couple also argued over ownership of their prized boat. This time Harding reported to police that Gillooly had threatened her over the issue. "I think we should break your legs and end your career," was the way Harding reported Gillooly's threat to police.

As their final divorce papers went through in the fall of 1993, there was another reconciliation, against the advice of both families. Legally, at least, they were finally divorced. Harding, who previously went by the name Harding Gillooly, asked reporters to drop her husband's last name at the Skate America competition. In October, in the Portland suburb of Milwaukee, another argument reportedly broke out while Gillooly was moving Harding's belongings back to their home to end the separation. A resident reported that Harding and her husband were involved in some sort of gunplay in a parking lot. Harding admitted that a gun had gone off in her hands but said the firing was accidental. Nobody was hurt in that incident, and no charges were filed by police.

Through all the tough years, Gillooly rarely gave Harding much monetary support. He filled warehouse orders for the Oregon Liquor Control Commission for a while, then left to manage her career. His financial future was wrapped up in Harding's success. He could usually be sighted at competitions, pacing the ice rink or the stands nervously while his wife was competing. In Detroit he was still there, helping to sell merchandise and to set up Harding's promotional schedule.

Harding did not always need Gillooly to get into trouble. After a car accident in Portland in 1992, she threatened the other driver with a baseball bat. "A whiffle ball bat," she later pointed out defensively.

Her stepfather, James Golden, told *Newsweek* that Harding "was very selfish, very surly." If she hadn't projected that image, said Golden, "she'd have been on top a long time ago—and stayed there."

Harding never got there, and part of the problem was that judges and potential sponsors simply didn't trust her disposition. Her coach, Diane Rawlinson, was one of the most respected and admired figures in the sport. Harding basically fired Rawlinson in 1989, then hired her back when her performances fell apart. Rawlinson still admired Harding for what she had made of herself. "You just know with Tonya she is always going to do things her way," Rawlinson said.

One of the things that Harding did, for a while, was to stick with Gillooly after the attack. Her loyalty made no sense from a strategic standpoint. Gillooly was deeply implicated in the crime. Harding was still on the periphery of the investigation. Yet she stayed with him in the same cabin outside Portland, professing his innocence. The rocky couple was filmed together by the television cameras. It became hard to believe that one would know something and the other might not.

"You have to understand, for both of them, the periods when they were apart were very empty," said Mark Anderson, a mutual friend and neighbor who had known Gillooly for fifteen years. "It wouldn't surprise me, after all this was over, if they got married again."

After a week of solid support, however, Harding dumped Gillooly, leaving him bitter again. The *Detroit News* reported that Gillooly was "trying to cut a deal." The paper said that Gillooly had told investigators he could serve her up "on a silver platter." This was a long way from the Gillooly of just one week earlier, who had told reporters, "I have too much faith in my wife's ability to bump off the competition."

Harding kept skating at the Clackamas Town Center Shopping Mall, aiming for the Olympics. Shoppers at the mall stopped, stared, and applauded her more difficult moves. Although film crews were quick to show every stumble on national television, Harding's skating appeared fairly sharp; it was just her image that had taken a terrible beating. She was now a running joke on every late night television show and every radio talk show. Howard Stern, the syndicated radio shock jock, mocked her frizzy hair and the hours of make-overs that he said had not helped Harding look like a bona fide figure skater. He called her skating outfits "Halloween costumes."

The Tonya Harding Fan Club, with its five hundred members in and around Portland, stood behind her with a religious fervor. But Harding's reputation, and her marketability, could not have slipped any lower.

"She is absolutely dead," David Burns of the Burns Sports Celebrity Service told the *New York Daily News*. "Advertisers do not want to be associated with negatives like this. It's really very sad."

Harding was part of the story—Kerrigan's story. If Harding was going to cash in, it would only be as Kerrigan's evil twin. Major Broadcasting, Inc., a Chicago-based media company, actually began preliminary discussions with representatives of both Kerrigan and Harding about a possible $5 million winner-take-all post-Olympic competition. The chances for such a duel seemed remote, and Harding's chances for winning it were even more so. Not only did Kerrigan skate a better overall program than Harding, she was now the heroine in a giant soap opera.

Everybody was fascinated by the ice escapades. Everyone tried to put the fiasco in a larger context. There had to be something more to this, something beyond a group of incompetent thugs bumbling a hit on an Olympic athlete. Athletes shook their heads. They could not imagine how one athlete's camp could sabotage another athlete. It went against everything sports was supposed to represent. There was never a competitive tale like this one, with the possible exception of the Texas mother who tried to knock off a high school student so her own daughter could make the cheerleading squad.

"When I was playing, the most you'd do is

hope the other player loses before you had to play her," said Chris Evert, who for a decade waged more sensible tennis wars with Martina Navratilova.

"The underlying theme is still about being number one, and what goes along with that," Evert said. "The emphasis always was there on that. When I was number one, everyone wanted me. When I was number two, I was a better player and a more interesting person. But people treated me like chopped liver. I haven't read much about Arantxa Sanchez or Tonya Harding before this," Evert said. "You don't hype number two or number three. That's Wall Street and commercialism."

Evert is right; there's nothing new about the national obsession with being first. It's just this: Whoever imagined the obsession would be taken to such an unfathomable extreme?

Epilogue:
Lillehammer and Beyond

Stardom has long been a doubled-edged sword to Nancy Kerrigan. It has enabled her to sign endorsement deals with an array of different sponsors, generating income believed to be in the high six figures. It has brought her fame and even adoration. But it is also something she can be profoundly uncomfortable about. Remember how bashful she was after signing on with Seiko at the U.S. Nationals in Phoenix in 1993, not knowing quite what to say or do? This is the way she has always been known at Stoneham Arena, at Hank's Bakery, and up and down Cedar Avenue.

"She's just a very low-key girl," said Ducky Antonucci, the Stoneham skating instructor. "I think she just wants to be left alone to do her own thing."

Theresa Martin, who started her on her way, said, "I truly think she's just a down-to-earth person who has this amazing skill."

Her skill, her luminous looks, and the most famous right knee in America have combined to catapult Nancy Kerrigan into a spotlight she never imagined. It was abundantly clear that she would emerge from the Winter Olympic's a bigger star than ever, a scary thought for a basically shy young woman who had film crews camped out at the edge of her driveway for weeks. There was always something special about her allure. Now, a crude iron bar across the knee had lifted her beyond that, to another realm in the thoughts and esteem of people in America and even around the world. The glare at the Olympics would be excruciating, of course, but the flip side was that millions would be rooting for her as few have ever been rooted for.

"That means so much to an athlete," said Carol Heiss Jenkins, the 1960 gold medalist and a prominent coach, speaking to the *New York Daily News*. "It would be such a plus for Nancy if she can look at it that way. She's going to get a standing ovation when she comes out there. Everyone will be saying 'We're with you all the way. We're going to do all we can to support you.' If she can just tell herself that no matter what she does, everybody is for her, I think it can be such a positive thing. I hope she has a wonderful time out there. With all that support, I hope that she can just go out there and think about skating her best, and doing it to please herself, because that's where it has to start."

Nancy Kerrigan has transcended her own sport and possibly all sports. She represents the victim as survivor, and possibly as conquerer. As a January in Stoneham turned into February in Norway, Nancy Kerrigan was already a champion. She didn't really need a medal around her neck to prove it.

A Viewer's Guide to Figure Skating

Figure skating is a sport decided by judges, whose scoring can appear almost arbitrary at times. More often than not, however, there is method to their marks. If you know what to look for, and listen to the color analyst, you can probably project scores with a fair amount of accuracy.

The technical program, which lasts about two minutes and forty seconds, counts for one-third of the final standing for both the men and women. The technical programs have certain required elements. Among these are jumps, spins, step sequences, and a set combination of jumps interrupted only by a brief landing. If the skater fails to complete any of these elements, he or she will be penalized on technical marks. Falling to the ice generally costs a skater at least two-tenths of a point in technical marks, but some consideration is given to degree of difficulty. The same is true for "popping" or "stepping out" of a jump, when a skater does not complete the scheduled number of rotations.

In the long program—four minutes for the women, four and a half for the men—judges look for variety of jumps as well as quantity. If a skater such as Surya Bonaly completes four different kinds of triple jumps, she will be given more credit than another skater who simply completes four triple-toe loops. Each type of jump involves landing and taking off on different edges of narrow, concave blades. Each one is a different, learned skill, but only experts can tell the difference between most jumps. Only the axel is obvious, because it is the one jump in which the skater takes off while facing forward. Six years ago, at the Calgary Olympics, most women were attempting only three triples. Now, to be competitive, top women must attempt five or six triples.

Marks range up to 6.0 for both technical merit and artistic interpretation. Artistic marks are more subjective, based on line, pacing, and interpretation of music. Judges like to see a skater spread out his or her jumps over the course of a program. It is considered poor form to stick all the toughest moves in the front end, then coast the rest of the way. Brian Boitano redesigned his Olympic program at the suggestion of judges who objected to a quiet, restful minute in the middle. He took out a slow, artistic hairpin turn. He put in another jump.

The most common misconception among viewers is that a low score from a judge is a bad thing for a skater. The situation is more complicated than that, because the scoring from the nine judges is based on ordinals. Some judges just score everyone lower. Each judge carefully ranks the skaters relative to each other, leaving some room at the top. For example, the Canadian judge gives Nancy Kerrigan only a 5.3 in technical and artistic scores but gives Oksana Baiul 5.2's and Bonaly 5.1's. Kerrigan receives a number one ordinal from this judge, Baiul a two and Bonaly a three. The sum of the ordinals from the nine judges determines the final placement, with the lowest ordinal total winning the gold medal.

A first-place finish in the long program assures a first-place finish overall, as long as the skater was no lower than third after the technical program. Reputation certainly counts with the judges, but not as much as it once did. Cold War judging blocs are no longer in existence. Skaters are no longer required to etch compulsory figures in near private sessions, which was once a subjective playground for judges. Now performing takes place before a crowd, and judges must answer to the cheers, the jeers, and a television audience ready to be outraged.

Glossary of Figure Skating Terms

ACCOUNTANT: An official at a competition who tallies marks awarded by judges and then determines who placed where.

AXEL JUMP: Named for its inventor, Axel Paulsen, this is the only jump in which the skater takes off from a forward position. A single axel consists of 1½ revolutions, a double axel 2½ revolutions, and a triple axel 3½. Widely regarded as among the most difficult jumps in skating.

CROSSOVERS: A technique skaters use to gain speed and turn corners, which involves crossing one foot over the other. Crossovers are done going both forward and backward.

DEATH SPIRAL: A move performed by pairs where the man spins in a pivot as he holds a hand of the woman, who is spinning horizontally with her body parallel to the ice.

FLIP JUMP: A toe-pick-assisted jump in which the skater takes off from the back inside edge of one foot and lands on the back outside edge of the other foot.

FREE SKATE: A synonym for long program, the free skate accounts for 66⅔ percent of the skater's final score. Because there are no required elements, skaters are free to select music, theme, and choreography and perform whatever routine they believe will best showcase their skills. Men skate a four-and-one-half-minute-long program, women four minutes.

HAND-TO-HAND LOOP LIFT: A pairs move in which the man raises his partner over his head, with the partner in front of him and facing the same direction. She stays in the same direction in a sitting position with hands behind her, while her partner supports her by the hands.

HYDRANT LIFT: A move in which the man throws his partner over his head while skating backward, rotates one-half turn, and catches her as she's facing him.

JUMP COMBINATION: Putting different jumps together in a way that the landing edge of one jump serves as the takeoff edge for the next jump.

KISS AND CRY AREA: The colloquial name for the area where skaters and their coaches wait for their marks to flash on the scoreboard.

LATERAL TWIST: A move in which the man throws his partner overhead, where she rotates once while parallel to the ice and is then caught.

LAYBACK SPIN: An upright spin performed by

women (usually) in which the head and shoulders are dropped backward and the back is arched.

LIFTS: General term for pair moves in which the man lifts his partner over his head.

LONG PROGRAM: Same as **FREE SKATE.**

LOOP: A jump in which the skater takes off from a back outside edge and lands on the same edge.

LUTZ: A jump assisted by the toe pick where the skater takes off from a back outside edge and lands on the back outside edge of the opposite foot.

ORDINALS: The scores given to skaters according to their placement by individual judges. A skater earns an ordinal of one from a judge if she earned the highest marks from that judge; an ordinal of two, if ranked second. The ordinals from all nine judges are then totaled. The lower the total, the better the final standing.

PLATTER LIFT: A pairs move in which the man hoists his partner overhead, his hands resting on her hips. She remains horizontal to the ice, facing the back of the man, in a platter position.

SALCHOW: An edge jump in which the skater takes off from the back inside edge of one foot and lands on the back outside edge of the opposite foot. Named for its creator, Ulrich Salchow.

SHADOW SKATING: Any move in pair skating where both partners move in sync while in close proximity.

SHORT PROGRAM: The technical part of the singles and pairs competition. Lasting for two minutes, forty seconds, it consists of eight elements that must be completed. Skaters are penalized if they fail to execute the required moves.

SIT SPIN: A spin done in a sitting position, with the body low to the ice and the skating knee bent, while the nonskating leg is extended beside it.

STAR LIFT: A lift in which the man raises his partner by her hip, from the side. She is in the scissors position, either touching his shoulder with her hand or having no hands on him at all.

TECHNICAL PROGRAM: See **SHORT PROGRAM.**

THROW JUMP: A jump in which the male helps lift the lady into the air, then executes one, two, or three revolutions and lands skating backward.

TOE LOOP: A jump assisted by the toe pick in which the skater takes off and lands on the same back outside edge.

TOE PICKS: The teeth at the front of the skate blade that enable skater to jump and spin.

Nancy Kerrigan:
At a Glance

BORN: October 13, 1969 Woburn, Mass.
HEIGHT: 5 feet 4 inches
WEIGHT: 111 lbs.
HOME CLUB: Colonial Figure Skating Club
HOMETOWN: Stoneham, Mass.
COACHES: Evy and Mary Scotvold
CHOREOGRAPHERS: Mary Scotvold, Mark Militano

COMPETITIVE RESULTS

1994 U.S.Nationals	Did not compete
1993 AT&T Pro-Am	1st
1993 Piruetten	1st
1993 Hershey's Kisses Pro Am	2nd

1993 World Championships	5th
1992 U.S. Nationals	1st
1992 Chrysler Concorde Pro-Am Challenge	1st
1992 Skate America	2nd
1992 World Championships	2nd
1992 Olympic Games	3rd
1992 U.S. Nationals	2nd
1991 Nations Cup	1st
1991 Trophy Lalique	3rd
1991 World Championships	3rd
1991 U.S. Nationals	3rd
1990 Trophy Lalique	3rd
1990 Goodwill Games	5th
1990 U.S. Olympic Festival	1st
1990 U.S. Nationals	4th
1989 U.S. Olympic Festival	3rd
1989 World University Games (Sofia, Bulgaria)	3rd
1989 National Senior	5th
1989 Eastern Senior	1st
1989 New England Senior	1st
1988 Novarat Trophy (Budapest, Hungary)	1st

1988 Carl Schafer Memorial (Vienna, Austria)	1st
1988 National Collegiates	1st
1988 National Senior	12th
1987 NHK Trophy (Kushiro, Japan)	5th
1987 Olympic Festival	2nd (team)
1987 National Junior	4th
1987 Eastern Junior	2nd
1987 New England Junior	3rd
1986 National Junior	11th
1986 Eastern Junior	4th
1986 New England Junior	2nd
1985 National Junior	11th
1985 Eastern Junior	2nd

UNITED STATES
FIGURE SKATING CHAMPIONSHIPS

MEN'S SINGLES

	GOLD	SILVER	BRONZE
1914 New Haven, CT	Norman M. Scott	Edward Howland	Nathaniel Niles
1915–1917	No Competition Held		
1918 New York, NY	Nathaniel Niles	Karl Engel	Edward Howland
1919	No Competition Held		
1920 New York, NY	Sherwin Badger	Nathaniel Niles	Petros Wahlman
1921 Philadelphia, PA	Sherwin Badger	Nathaniel Niles	Edward Howland
1922 Boston, MA	Sherwin Badger	Nathaniel Niles	—
1923 New Haven, CT	Sherwin Badger	Chris Christenson	Julius Nelson
1924 Philadelphia, PA	Sherwin Badger	Nathaniel Niles	Chris Christenson
1925 New York, NY	Nathaniel Niles	George Braakman	Carl Engel
1926 Boston, MA	Chris Christenson	Nathaniel Niles	Ferrier Martin
1927 New York, NY	Nathaniel Niles	Roger Turner	George Braakman
1928 New Haven, CT	Roger Turner	Fredrick Goodridge	W. Langer
1929 New York, NY	Roger Turner	Fredrick Goodridge	J. Lester Madden
1930 Providence, RI	Roger Turner	J. Lester Madden	George Hill
1931 Boston, MA	Roger Turner	J. Lester Madden	George Hill
1932 New York, NY	Roger Turner	J. Lester Madden	G. Borden
1933 New Haven, CT	Roger Turner	J. Lester Madden	Robin Lee
1934 Philadelphia, PA	Roger Turner	Robin Lee	George Hill

	GOLD	SILVER	BRONZE
1935 New Haven, CT	Robin Lee	Roger Turner	J. Lester Madden
1936 New York, NY	Robin Lee	Erie Reiter	George Hill
1937 Chicago, IL	Robin Lee	Erie Reiter	William Nagle
1938 Philadelphia, PA	Robin Lee	Erie Reiter	Ollie Haupt, Jr.
1939 St. Paul, MN	Robin Lee	Ollie Haupt, Jr.	Eugene Turner
1940 Cleveland, OH	Eugene Turner	Ollie Haupt, Jr.	Skippy Baxter
1941 Boston, MA	Eugene Turner	Arthur Vaughn	William Nagle
1942 Chicago, IL	Bobby Specht	William Grimditch	Arthur Vaughn
1943 New York, NY	Arthur Vaughn	Arthur Preusch	William Nagle
1944–45	**No Competition Held**		
1946 Chicago, IL	Richard Button	James Lochead	John Tuckerman
1947 Berkeley, CA	Richard Button	John Lettengarver	James Grogan
1948 Colorado Springs, CO	Richard Button	James Crogan	John Lettengarver
1949 Colorado Springs, CO	Richard Button	James Crogan	Hayes A. Jenkins
1950 Washington, D.C.	Richard Button	Hayes A. Jenkins	Richard Dwyer
1951 Seattle, WA	Richard Button	James Grogan	Hayes A. Jenkins
1952 Colorado Springs, CO	Richard Button	James Grogan	Hayes A. Jenkins
1953 Hershey, PA	Hayes A. Jenkins	Ronald Robertson	Dudley Richards
1954 Los Angeles, CA	Hayes A. Jenkins	David Jenkins	Ronald Robertson
1955 Colorado Springs, CO	Hayes A. Jenkins	David Jenkins	Hugh Graham

	GOLD	SILVER	BRONZE
1956 Philadelphia, PA	Hayes A. Jenkins	Ronald Robertson	David Jenkins
1957 Berkeley, CA	David Jenkins	Tim Brown	Tom Moore
1958 Minneapolis, MN	David Jenkins	Tim Brown	Tom Moore
1959 Rochester, NY	David Jenkins	Tim Brown	Robert Brewer
1960 Seattle, WA	David Jenkins	Tim Brown	Robert Brewer
1961 Colorado Springs, CO	Bradley Lord	Gregory Kelley	Tim Brown
1962 Boston, MA	Monty Hoyt	Scott Allen	David Edwards
1963 Long Beach, CA	Thomas Litz	Scott Allen	Monty Hoyt
1964 Cleveland, OH	Scott Allen	Thomas Litz	Monty Hoyt
1965 Lake Placid, NY	Gary Visconti	Scott Allen	Tim Wood
1966 Berkeley, CA	Scott Allen	Gary Visconti	Billy Chapel
1967 Omaha, NE	Gary Visconti	Scott Allen	Tim Wood
1968 Philadelphia, PA	Tim Wood	Gary Visconti	J. Misha Petkevich
1969 Seattle, WA	Tim Wood	J. Misha Petkevich	Gary Visconti
1970 Tulsa, OK	Tim Wood	J. Misha Petkevich	Kenneth Shelley
1971 Buffalo, NY	J. Misha Petkevich	Kenneth Shelly	Gordon McKellen
1972 Long Beach, CA	Kenneth Shelley	J. Misha Petkevich	Gordon McKellen
1973 Minneapolis, MN	Gordon McKellen	Robert Bradshaw	David Santee
1974 Providence, RI	Gordon McKellen	Terry Kubicka	Charles Tickner
1975 Oakland, CA	Gordon McKellen	Terry Kubicka	Charles Tickner
1976 Colorado Springs, CO	Terry Kubicka	David Santee	Scott Cramer

	GOLD	SILVER	BRONZE
1977 Hartford, CT	Charles Tickner	Scott Cramer	David Santee
1978 Portland, OR	Charles Tickner	David Santee	Scott Hamilton
1979 Cincinnati, OH	Charlest Tickner	Scott Cramer	David Santee
1980 Atlanta, GA	Charles Tickner	David Santee	Scott Hamilton
1981 San Diego, CA	Scott Hamilton	David Santee	Robert Wagenhoffer
1982 Indianapolis, IN	Scott Hamilton	Robert Wagenhoffer	David Santee
1983 Pittsburgh, PA	Scott Hamilton	Brian Boitano	Mark Cockerell
1984 Salt Lake City, UT	Scott Hamilton	Brian Boitano	Mark Cockerell
1985 Kansas City, MO	Brian Boitano	Mark Cockerell	Scott Williams
1986 Long Island, NY	Brian Boitano	Scott Williams	Daniel Doran
1987 Tacoma, WA	Brian Boitano	Christopher Bowman	Scott Williams
1988 Denver, CO	Brian Boitano	Paul Wylie	Christopher Bowman
1989 Baltimore, MD	Christopher Bowman	Daniel Doran	Paul Wylie
1990 Salt Lake City, UT	Todd Eldredge	Paul Wylie	Mark Mitchell
1991 Minneapolis, MN	Todd Eldredge	Christopher Bowman	Paul Wylie
1992 Orlando, FL	Christopher Bowman	Paul Wylie	Mark Mitchell
1993 Phoenix, AZ	Scott Davis	Mark Mitchell	Michael Chack

UNITED STATES
FIGURE SKATING CHAMPIONSHIPS

LADIES' SINGLES

	GOLD	SILVER	BRONZE
1914 New Haven, CT	Theresa Weld	Edith Rotch	Raynham Townshend

	GOLD	SILVER	BRONZE
1915–1917	**No Competition Held**		
1918 New York, NY	Rosemary Beresford	Theresa Weld	—
1919	**No Competition Held**		
1920 New York, NY	Theresa Weld	Martha Brown	Lillian Cramer
1921 Philadelphia, PA	Theresa Blanchard	Lillian Cramer	—
1922 Boston, MA	Theresa Blanchard	Beatrix Loughran	—
1923 New Haven, CT	Theresa Blanchard	Beatrix Loughran	Lillian Cramer
1924 Philadelphia, PA	Theresa Blanchard	Rosalie Knapp	—
1925 New York, NY	Beatrix Loughran	Theresa Blanchard	Rosalie Knapp
1926 Boston, MA	Beatrix Loughran	Theresa Blanchard	Maribel Vinson
1927 New York, NY	Beatrix Loughran	Maribel Vinson	Theresa Blanchard
1928 New Haven	Maribel Vinson	Suzanne Davis	—
1929 New York, NY	Maribel Vinson	Edith Secord	Suzanne Davis
1930 Providence, RI	Maribel Vinson	Edith Secord	Suzanne Davis
1931 Boston, MA	Maribel Vinson	Edith Secord	Hulda Berger
1932 New York, NY	Maribel Vinson	Margaret Bennett	Louise Weigel
1933 New Haven, CT	Maribel Vinson	Suzanne Davis	Louise Weigel
1934 Philadelphia, PA	Suzanne Davis	Louise Weigel	Estelle Weigel
1935 New Haven, CT	Maribel Vinson	Suzanne Davis	Louise Weigel
1936 New York, NY	Maribel Vinson	Louise Weigel	Audrey Peppe
1937 Chicago, IL	Maribel Vinson	Polly Blodgett	Katherine Durbrow
1938 Philadelphia, PA	Joan Tozzer	Audrey Peppe	Polly Blodgett

	GOLD	**SILVER**	**BRONZE**
1939 St. Paul, MI	Joan Tozzer	Audrey Peppe	Charlotte Walther
1940 Cleveland, OH	Joan Tozzer	Heddy Stenuf	Jane Vaughn
1941 Boston, MA	Jane Vaughn	Gretchen Merrill	Charlotte Walther
1942 Chicago, IL	Jane Vaughn	Gretchen Merrill	Phebe Tucker
1943 New York, NY	Gretchen Merrill	Dorothy Goos	Janette Ahrens
1944 Minneapolis, MN	Gretchen Merrill	Dorothy Goos	Ramona Allen
1945 New York, NY	Gretchen Merrill	Janette Ahrens	Madelon Olson
1946 Chicago, IL	Gretchen Merrill	Janette Ahrens	Madelon Olson
1947 Berkeley, CA	Gretchen Merrill	Janette Ahrens	Eileen Seigh
1948 Colorado Springs, CO	Gretchen Merrill	Yvonne C. Sherman	Helen Uhl
1949 Colorado Springs, CO	Yvonne C. Sherman	Gretchen Merrill	Virginia Baxter
1950 Washington, D.C.	Yvonne C. Sherman	Sonya Klopfer	Virginia Baxter
1951 Seattle, WA	Sonya Klopfer	Tenley Albright	Virginia Baxter
1952 Colorado Springs, CO	Tenley Albright	Frances Dorsey	Helen Geekie
1953 Hershey, PA	Tenley Albright	Carol Heiss	Margaret Graham
1954 Los Angeles, CA	Tenley Albright	Carol Heiss	Frances Dorsey
1955 Colorado Springs, CO	Tenley Albright	Carol Albright	Catherine Machado
1956 Philadelphia, PA	Tenley Albright	Carol Heiss	Catherine Machado
1957 Berkeley, CA	Carol Heiss	Joan Schenke	Claralynn Lewis

	GOLD	SILVER	BRONZE
1958 Minneapolis, MN	Carol Heiss	Carol Wanek	Lynn Finnegan
1959 Rochester, NY	Carol Heiss	Nancy Heiss	Barbara Roles
1960 Seattle, WA	Carol Heiss	Barbara Roles	Laurence Owen
1961 Colorado Springs, CO	Laurence Owen	Stephanie Westerfeld	Rhode L. Michelson
1962 Boston, MA	Barbara Roles	Lorraine Hanlon	Victoria Fisher
1963 Long Beach, CA	Lorraine Hanlon	Christine Haigler	Karen Howland
1964 Cleveland, Ohio	Peggy Fleming	Albertina Noyes	Christine Haigler
1965 Lake Placid, NY	Peggy Fleming	Christine Haigler	Albertina Noyes
1966 Berkeley, CA	Peggy Fleming	Albertina Noyes	Pamela Schneider
1967 Omaha, NE	Peggy Fleming	Albertina Noyes	Jennie Walsh
1968 Philadelphia, PA	Peggy Fleming	Albertina Noyes	Janet Lynn
1969 Seattle, WA	Janet Lynn	Julie Holmes	Albertina Noyes
1970 Tulsa, OK	Janet Lynn	Julie Holmes	Dawn Glab
1971 Buffalo, NY	Janet Lynn	Julie Holmes	Suna Murray
1972 Long Beach, CA	Janet Lynn	Julie Holmes	Suna Murray
1973 Minneapolis, MN	Janet Lynn	Dorothy Hamill	Jill McKinstry
1974 Providence, RI	Dorothy Hamill	Juli McKinstry	Kath Malmberg
1975 Oakland, CA	Dorothy Hamill	Wendy Burge	Kath Malmberg
1976 Colorado Springs, CO	Dorothy Hamill	Linda Fratianne	Wendy Burge
1977 Hartford, CT	Linda Fratianne	Barbie Smith	Wendy Burge

	GOLD	SILVER	BRONZE
1978 Portland, OR	Linda Fratianne	Lisa-Marie Allen	Priscilla Hill
1979 Cincinnati, OH	Linda Fratianne	Lisa-Marie Allen	Carrie Rugh
1980 Atlanta, GA	Linda Fratianne	Lisa-Marie Allen	Sandy Lenz
1981 San Diego, CA	Elaine Zayak	Priscilla Hill	Lisa-Marie Allen
1982 Indianpolis, IN	Rosalynn Sumners	Vikki de Vries	Elaine Zayak
1983 Pittsburgh, PA	Rosalynn Sumners	Elaine Zayak	Tiffany Chin
1984 Salt Lake City, UT	Rosalynn Sumners	Tiffany Chin	Elaine Zayak
1985 Kansas City, MO	Tiffany Chin	Debi Thomas	Caryn Kadavy
1986 Long Island, NY	Debi Thomas	Caryn Kadavy	Tiffany Chin
1987 Tacoma, WA	Jill Trenary	Debi Thomas	Caryn Kadavy
1988 Denver, CO	Debi Thomas	Jill Trenary	Caryn Kadavy
1989 Baltimore, MD	Jill Trenary	Kristi Yamaguchi	Tonya Harding
1990 Salt Lake City, UT	Jill Trenary	Kristi Yamaguchi	Holly Cook
1991 Minneapolis, MN	Tonya Harding	Kristi Yamaguchi	Nancy Kerrigan
1992 Orlando, FL	Kristi Yamaguchi	Nancy Kerrigan	Tonya Harding
1993 Phoenix, AZ	Nancy Kerrigan	Lisa Ervin	Tonia Kwiatkowski

UNITED STATES
FIGURE SKATING CHAMPIONSHIPS

PAIRS

	GOLD	SILVER	BRONZE
1914 New Haven, CT	Jeanne Chevalier Norman M. Scott	Theresa Weld Nathaniel Niles	Eleanor Crocker Edward Howland

	GOLD	SILVER	BRONZE
1915–1917	**No competition Held**		
1918 New York, NY	Theresa Weld Nathaniel Niles	Clara Frothingham Sherwin Badger	— —
1919	**No Competition Held**		
1920 New York, NY	Theresa Weld Nathaniel Niles	Edith Rotch Sherwin Badger	— —
1921 Philadelphia, PA	Theresa Blanchard Nathaniel Niles	Mrs. Edward Howland Mr. Edward Howland	Channing Frothingham Charles Rotch
1922 Boston, MA	Theresa Blanchard Nathaniel Niles	Mrs. Edward Howland Mr. Edward Howland	Edith Rotch Francis Munroe
1923 New Haven, CT	Theresa Blanchard Nathaniel Niles	— —	— —
1924 Philadelphia, PA	Theresa Blanchard Nathaniel Niles	Grace Munstock Joel Liberman	— —
1925 New York, NY	Theresa Blanchard Nathaniel Niles	Ada Bauman George Braakman	Grace Munstock Joel Liberman
1926 Boston, MA	Theresa Blanchard Nathaniel Niles	Sydney Good James Greene	Grace Munstock Joel Liberman
1927 New York, NY	Theresa Blanchard Nathaniel Niles	Beatrix Loughran Raymond Harvey	Ada Bauman George Braakman
1928 New Haven, CT	Maribel Vinson Thornton Coolidge	Theresa Blanchard Nathaniel Niles	Ada Bauman George Braakman
1929 New York, NY	Maribel Vinson Thornton Coolidge	Theresa Blanchard Nathaniel Niles	Edith Secord Joseph Savage
1930 Providence, RI	Beatrix Loughran Sherwin Badger	Maribel Vinson George Hill	Edith Secord Joseph Savage
1931 Boston, MA	Beatrix Loughran Sherwin Badger	Maribel Vinson George Hill	Grace Madden J. Lester Madden
1932 New York, NY	Beatrix Loughran Sherwin Badger	Maribel Vinson George Hill	G. Meredith Joseph Savage
1933 New Haven, CT	Maribel Vinson George Hill	Grace Madden J. Lester Madden	G. Meredith Joseph Savage

	GOLD	SILVER	BRONZE
1934 Philadelphia, PA	Grace Madden J. Lester Madden	Eva Schwerdt William Bruns	— —
1935 New Haven, CT	Maribel Vinson George Hill	Grace Madden J. Lester Madden	Eva Schwerdt William Bruns, Jr.
1936 New York, NY	Maribel Vinson George Hill	Polly Blodgett Roger Turner	Majorie Parker Howard Meredith
1937 Chicago, IL	Maribel Vinson George Hill	Grace Madden J. Lester Madden	Joan Tozzer Bernard Fox
1938 Philadelphia, PA	Joan Tozzer Bernard Fox	Grace Madden J. Lester Madden	Ardelle Sanderson Roland Janson
1939 St. Paul, MN	Joan Tozzer Bernard Fox	Annah M. Hall William Hall	Eva Bruns William Bruns
1940 Cleveland, OH	Joan Tozzer Bernard Fox	Heddy Stenuf Skippy Baxter	Eva Bruns William Bruns
1941 Boston, MA	Donna Atwood Eugene Turner	Patricia Vaeth Jack Might	Joan Mitchell Bobby Specht
1942 Chicago, IL	Doris Schubach Walter Noffke	Janette Ahrens Robert Uppgren	Margaret Field Jack Might
1943 New York, NY	Doris Schubach Walter Noffke	Janette Ahrens Robert Uppgren	Dorothy Goos Edward LeMaire
1944 Minneapolis, MN	Doris Schubach Walter Noffke	Janette Ahrens Arthur Preusch	Marcella May James Lochead
1945 New York, NY	Donna J. Pospisil Jean P. Brunet	Ann McGean Michael McGean	Marcella M. Willis James Lochead
1946 Chicago, IL	Donna J. Pospisil Jean P. Brunet	Karol Kennedy Peter Kennedy	Patty Sonnekson Charles Brinkman
1947 Berkeley, CA	Yvonne Sherman Robert Swenning	Karol Kennedy Peter Kennedy	Carolyn Welch Charles Brinkman
1948 Colorado Springs, CO	Karol Kennedy Peter Kennedy	Yvonne Sherman Robert Swenning	Harriet Sutton Lyman Wakefield
1949 Colorado Springs, CO	Karol Kennedy Peter Kennedy	Irene Maguire Walter Muehlbronner	Anne Davies Carleton Hoffner
1950 Washington, D.C.	Karol Kennedy Peter Kennedy	Irene Maguire Walter Muehlbronner	Anne Davies Carleton Hoffner
1951 Seattle, WA	Karol Kennedy Peter Kennedy	Janet Gerhauser John Nightingale	Anne Holt Austin Holt
1952 Colorado Springs, CO	Karol Kennedy Peter Kennedy	Janet Gerhauser John Nightingale	— —

	GOLD	SILVER	BRONZE
1953 Hershey, PA	Carole Ormaca Robin Greiner	Margaret A. Graham Hugh C. Graham	Kay Servatius Sully Kothman
1954 Los Angeles, CA	Carole Ormaca Robin Greiner	Margaret A. Graham Hugh C. Graham	Lucille Ash Sully Kothman
1955 Colorado Springs, CO	Carole Ormaca Robin Greiner	Lucille Ash Sully Kothman	Agnes Tyson Richard Swenning
1956 Philadelphia, PA	Carol Ormaca Robin Greiner	Lucille Ash Sully Kothman	Maribel Owen Charles Foster
1957 Berkeley, CA	Nancy Rouillard Ronald Ludington	Mary J. Watson John Jarmon	Anita Tefkin James Barlow
1958 Minneapolis, MN	Nancy Ludington Ronald Ludington	Sheila Wells Robin Greiner	Maribel Owen Dudley Richards
1959 Rochester, NY	Nancy Ludington Ronald Ludington	Gayle Freed Karl Freed	Maribel Owen Dudley Richards
1960 Seattle, WA	Nancy Ludington Ronald Ludington	Maribel Owen Dudley Richards	Ila Ray Hadley Ray Hadley, Jr.
1961 Colorado Springs, CO	Maribel Owen Dudley Richards	Ila Ray Hadley Ray Hadley, Jr.	Laurie Hickox William Hickox
1962 Boston, MA	Dorothyann Nelson Pieter Kollen	Judianne Fotheringill Jerry Fotheringill	Vivian Joseph Ronald Joseph
1963 Long Beach, CA	Judianne Fotheringill Jerry Fotheringill	Vivian Joseph Ronald Joseph	Patti Gustafson Pieter Kollen
1964 Cleveland, OH	Judianne Fotheringill Jerry Fotheringill	Vivian Joseph Ronald Joseph	Cynthia Kauffman Ronald Kauffman
1965 Lake Placid, NY	Vivian Joseph Ronald Joseph	Cynthia Kauffman Ronald Kauffman	Joanne Heckert Gary Clark
1966 Berkeley, CA	Cynthia Kauffman Ronald Kauffman	Susan Berens Roy Wagelein	Page Paulsen Larry Dusich
1967 Omaha, NE	Cynthia Kauffman Ronald Kauffman	Susan Berens Roy Wagelein	Betty Lewis Richard Gilbert
1968 Philadelphia, PA	Cynthia Kauffman Ronald Kauffman	Sandi Sweitzer Roy Wagelein	JoJo Starbuck Kenneth Shelley
1969 Seattle, WA	Cynthia Kauffman Ronald Kauffman	JoJo Starbuck Kenneth Shelley	Melissa Militano Mark Militano
1970 Tulsa, OK	JoJo Starbuck Kenneth Shelley	Melissa Militano Mark Militano	Sheri Thrapp Larry Dusich

	GOLD	SILVER	BRONZE
1971 Buffalo, NY	JoJo Starbuck Kenneth Shelley	Melissa Militano Mark Militano	Barbara Brown Doug Berndt
1972 Long Beach, CA	JoJo Starbuck Kenneth Shelley	Melissa Militano Mark Militano	Barbara Brown Doug Berndt
1973 Minneapolis, MN	Melissa Militano Mark Militano	Gale Fuhrman Joel Fuhrman	Emily Benenson Johnny Johns
1974 Providence, RI	Melissa Militano Johnny Johns	Tai Babilonia Randy Gardner	Erica Susman Thomas Huff
1975 Oakland, CA	Melissa Militano Johnny Johns	Tai Babilonia Randy Gardner	Emily Benenson Jack Courtney
1976 Colorado Springs, CO	Tai Babilonia Randy Gardner	Alice Cook William Fauver	Emily Benenson Jack Courtney
1977 Hartford, CT	Tai Babilonia Randy Gardner	Gail Hamula Frank Sweiding	Sheryl Franks Michael Botticelli
1978 Portland, OR	Tai Babilonia Randy Gardner	Gail Hamula Frank Sweiding	Sheryl Franks Michael Botticelli
1979 Cincinnati, OH	Tai Babilonia Randy Gardner	Vicki Heasley Robert Wagenhoffer	Sheryl Franks Michael Botticelli
1980 Atlanta, GA	Tai Babilonia Randy Gardner	Caitlin Carruthers Peter Carruthers	Sheryl Franks Michael Botticelli
1981 San Diego, CA	Caitlin Carruthers Peter Carruthers	Lea Ann Miller William Fauver	Beth Flora Ken Flora
1982 Indianapolis, IN	Caitlin Carruthers Peter Carruthers	Maria DiDomenico Burt Lancon	Lea Ann Miller William Fauver
1983 Pittsburgh, PA	Caitlin Carruthers Peter Carruthers	Lea Ann Miller William Fauver	Jill Watson Burt Lancon
1984 Salt Lake City, UT	Caitlin Carruthers Peter Carruthers	Lea Ann Miller William Fauver	Jill Watson Burt Lancon
1985 Kansas City, MO	Jill Watson Peter Oppegard	Natalie Seybold Wayne Seybold	Gillian Wachsman Todd Waggoner
1986 Long Island, NY	Gillian Wachsman Todd Waggoner	Jill Watson Peter Oppegard	Natalie Seybold Wayne Seybold
1987 Tacoma, WA	Jill Watson Peter Oppegard	Gillian Wachsman Todd Waggoner	Katy Keely Joseph Mero
1988 Denver, CO	Jill Watson Peter Oppegard	Gillian Wachsman Todd Waggoner	Natalie Seybold Wayne Seybold
1989 Baltimore, MD	Kristi Yamaguchi Rudi Galindo	Natalie Seybold Wayne Seybold	Katy Kelley Joseph Mero
1990 Salt Lake City, UT	Kristi Yamaguchi Rudi Galindo	Natasha Kuchiki Todd Sand	Sharon Carz Doug Williams

	GOLD	SILVER	BRONZE
1991 Minneapolis, MN	Natasha Kuchiki Todd Sand	Calla Urbanski Rocky Marval	Jenni Meno Scott Wendland
1992 Orlando, FL	Calla Urbanski Rocky Marval	Jenni Meno Scott Wendland	Natasha Kuchiki Todd Sand
1993 Phoenix, AZ	Calla Urbanski Rocky Marval	Jenni Meno Todd Sand	Karen Courtland R. Todd Reynolds

UNITED STATES
FIGURE SKATING CHAMPIONSHIPS

ICE DANCING

	GOLD	SILVER	BRONZE
1914 New Haven, CT Waltz	Theresa Weld Nathaniel Niles	Jeanne Chavalier Norman Scott	— —
1915–1919	**No Competition Held**		
1920 New York, NY Waltz	Theresa Weld Nathaniel Niles	Rosalie Dunn Joel Liberman	— —
Fourteen Step	Gertrude Cheever Porter Irving Brokaw	Rosalie Dunn Joel Liberman	— —
1921 Philadelphia, PA Waltz	Theresa Weld Blanchard Nathaniel Niles	Clara Frothingham Sherwin Badger	Virginia Slattery C.J. Cruikshank
Fourteen Step	Theresa Weld Blanchard Nathaniel Niles	Virginia Slattery C.J. Cruikshank	Mrs. Edward Howland Mr. Edward Howland —Tie— Clara Frothingham Charles Rotch
1922 Boston, MA Waltz	Beatrix Loughran Edward Howland	Theresa Weld Blanchard Nathaniel Niles	Mrs. Henry Howe Mr. Henry Howe
Fourteen Step	Theresa Weld Blanchard Nathaniel Niles	Mrs. Henry Howe Mr. Henry Howe	Ella Snelling Sherwin Badger

	GOLD	SILVER	BRONZE
1923			
New Haven, CT			
Waltz	Mrs. Henry Howe	Theresa Weld	Rosalie Dunn
	Mr. Henry Howe	Blanchard	Petros Wahlman
		Charles Rotch	
Fourteen Step	Sydney Goode	Theresa Weld	Rosalie Dunn
	James Greene	Blanchard	Petros Wahlman
		Nathaniel Niles	
1924			
Philadelphia, PA			
Waltz	Rosalie Dunn	Sydney Goode	Theresa Weld
	Fredrick Gabel	James Greene	Blanchard
			Nathaniel Niles
Fourteen Step	Sydney Goode	Theresa Weld	Clara Frothingham
	James Greene	Blanchard	Sherwin Badger
		Nathaniel Niles	
1925			
New York, NY			
Waltz	Virginia Slattery	Sydney Goode	Mrs. Henry Howe
	Ferrier Martin	James Green	Mr. Henry Howe
Fourteen Step	Virginia Slattery	Sydney Goode	Ada Baumann
	Ferrier Martin	James Greene	George Braakman
1926			
Boston, MA			
Waltz	Rosalie Dunn	Sydney Goode	Edna Gutterman
	Joseph Savage	James Greene	Frederick Gabel
Fourteen Step	Sydney Goode	Virginia Slattery	Edna Gutterman
	James Greene	Ferrier Martin	Frederick Gabel
1927			
New York, NY			
Waltz	Rosalie Dunn	Virginia Slattery	Martin Ada
	Joseph Savage	Ferrier Martin	Bauman
			George Braakman
Fourteen Step	Rosalie Dunn	Ada Baumann	Virginia Slattery
	Joseph Savage	George Braakman	Martin
			Ferrier Martin
1928			
New Haven, CT			
Waltz	Rosalie Dunn	Elsie Koscheck	Ada Baumann
	Joseph Savage	Frederick Gabel	Kelly
			George Braakman
Fourteen Step	Ada Baumann	Maribel Vinson	Rosalie Dunn
	Kelly	Lester Madden	Joseph Savage
	George Braakman		

	GOLD	SILVER	BRONZE
1929 New York, NY			
Waltz & Original Dance Combined	Edith Secord Joseph Savage	Theresa Weld Blanchard Nathaniel Niles	Maribel Vinson Lester Madden
1930 Providence, RI			
Waltz	Edith Secord Joseph Savage	Virginia Martin Ferrier Martin	Nettie Prantell Roy Hunt
Original Dance	Clara Frothingham George Hill	Edith Secord Joseph Savage	Theresa Weld Blanchard Nathaniel Niles
1931 Boston, MA			
Waltz	Edith Secord Ferrier Martin	Clara Frothingham Harold Hartshorne	— —
Original Dance	Theresa Weld Blanchard Nathaniel Niles	Edith Secord Ferrier Martin	Clara Frothingham George B. Hill
1932 New York, NY			
Waltz	Edith Secord Joseph Savage	Nettie Prantell Roy Hunt	Clara Frothingham Frederick Goodridge
Original Dance	Clara Frothingham George Hill	Edith Secord Joseph Savage	Theresa Weld Blanchard Nathaniel Niles
1933 New Haven, CT			
Waltz	Ilse Twaroschk Fred Fleischman	Eva Schwerdt William Burns	Miss Dutton Harold Hartshorne
Original Dance	Suzanne Davis Frederick Goodridge	Gertrude Meredith Joseph Savage	Grace Madden James Madden
1934 Philadelphia, PA			
Waltz	Nettie Prantell Roy Hunt	Ise Twaroschk Fred Fleischman	Eva Schwerdt William Bruns
Original Dance	Suzanne Davis Frederick Goodridge	Grade Madden Joseph Madden	Ruth English Len Fogassey

	GOLD	SILVER	BRONZE
1935 New Haven, CT Waltz*	Nettie Prantell Roy Hunt	Ilse Twaroschk Fred Fleischman	Maribel Vinson Joseph Savage

*Original Dance Competition was an exhibition in 1935 in anticipation of a new dance championship the following year

	GOLD	SILVER	BRONZE
1936 Boston, MA	Marjorie Parker Joseph Savage	Nettie Prantell Harold Hartshorne	Clara Frothingham Ashton Parmenter
1937 Chicago, IL	Nettie Prantell Harold Hartshorne	Marjorie Parker Joseph Savage	Ardelle Kloss Roland Jansea
1938 Philadelphia, PA	Nettie Prantel Harold Hartshorne	Katherine Durbrow Joseph Savage	Louise W. Atwell Otto Dallmayr
1939 St. Paul, MN	Sandy MacDonald Harold Hartshorne	Nettie Prantel Joseph Savage	Marjorie Parker George Boltres
1940 Cleveland, OH	Sandy MacDonald Harold Hartshorne	Nettie Prantel George Boltres	Vernafay Thysell Paul Harrington
1941 Boston, MA	Sandy MacDonald Harold Hartshorne	Elizabeth Kennedy Eugene Turner	Edith Whetstone A. I. Richards
1942 Chicago, IL	Edith Whetstone Alfred Richards	Sandy MacDonald Harold Hartshorne	Ramona Allen Herman Torrano
1943 New York, NY	Marcella May James Lochead	Majorie P. Smith Joseph Savage	Nettie Prantel Harold Hartshorne
1944 Minneapolis, MN	Marcella May James Lochead	Kathe Mehl Harold Hartshorne	Mary Andersen Jack Andersen
1945 New York, NY	Kathe Williams Robert Swenning	Marcella Willis James Lochead	Anne Davies Carleton Hoffner
1946 Chicago, IL	Anne Davies Carleton Hoffner	Lois Waring Walter Bainbridge	Carmel Waterbury Edward Bodel
1947 Berkeley, CA	Lois Waring Walter Bainbridge	Anne Davies Carleton Hoffner	Marcella Willis Frank Davenport
1948 Colorado Springs, CO	Lois Waring Walter Bainbridge	Anne Davies Carleton Hoffner	Irene Maguire Frank Davenport
1949 Colorado Springs, CO	Lois Waring Walter Bainbridge	Irene Maguire Walter Muehlbronner	Carmel Bodel Edward Bodel

	GOLD	SILVER	BRONZE
1950 Washington, D.C.	Lois Waring Michael McGean	Irene Macguire Walter Meuhlbronner	Anne Davies Carleton Hoffner
1951 Seattle, WA	Carmel Bodel Edward Bodel	Virginia Hoyns Donald Jacoby	Carol Ann Peters Daniel Ryan
1952 Colorado Springs, CO	Lois Waring Michael McGean	Carol Ann Peters Daniel Ryan	Carmel Bodel Edward Bodel
1953 Hershey, PA	Carol Ann Peters Daniel Ryan	Virginia Hoyns Donald Jacoby	Carmel Bodel Edward Bodel
1954 Los Angeles, CA	Carmel Bodel Edward Bodel	Phyllis Forney Martin Forney	Patsy Riedel Roland Junso
1955 Colorado Springs, CO	Carmel Bodel Edward Bodel	Joan Zamboni Roland Junso	Phyllis Forney Martin Forney
1956 Philadelphia, PA	Joan Zamboni Roland Junso	Carmel Bodel Edward Bodel	Sidney Arnold Franklin Nelson
1957 Berkeley, CA	Sharon McKenzie Bert Wright	Andree Anderson Donald Jacoby	Joan Zamboni Roland Junso
1958 Minneapolis, MN	Andree Anderson Donald Jacoby	Claire O'Neil John Bejshak	Susan Sebo Tim Brown
1959 Rochester, NY	Andree Jacoby Donald Jacoby	Margie Ackles Charles Phillips	Judy Ann Lamar Ronald Ludington
1960 Seattle, WA	Margie Ackles Charles Phillips	Marilyn Meeker Larry Pierce	Yvonne Littlefield Roger Campbell
1961 Colorado Springs, CO	Dianne Sherbloom Larry Pierce	Dona Lee Carrier Roger Campbell	Patricia Dineen Robert Dineen
1962 Boston, MA	Yvonne Littlefield Peter Betts	Dorothyann Nelson Pieter Kollen	Lorna Dyer King Cole
1963 Long Beach, CA	Sally Schantz Stanley Urban	Yvonne Littlefield Peter Betts	Lorna Dyer John Carrell
1964 Cleveland, OH	Darlene Streich Charles Fetter	Carole MacSween Robert Munz	Lorna Dyer John Carrell
1965 Lake Placid, NY	Kristin Fortune Dennis Sveum	Lorna Dyer John Carrell	Susan Urban Stanley Urban
1966 Berkeley, CA	Kristin Fortune Dennis Sveum	Lorna Dyer John Carrell	Susan urban Stanley Urban
1967 Omaha, NE	Lorna Dyer John Carrell	Alma Davenport Roger Berry	Judy Schwomeyer James Sladky
1968 Philadelphia, PA	Judy Schwomeyer James Sladky	Vicki Camper Eugene Heffron	Debbie Gerken Raymond Tiedtmann

	GOLD	SILVER	BRONZE
1969 Seattle, WA	Judy Schwomeyer James Sladky	Joan Bitterman Brad Hislop	Debbie Gerken Raymond Tiedemann
1970 Tulsa, OK	Judy Schwomeyer James Sladky	Anne Millier Harvey Millier	Debbie Ganson Brad Hislop
1971 Buffalo, NY	Judy Schwomeyer James Sladky	Anne Millier Harvey Millier	Mary Campbell Johnny Johns
1972 Long Beach, CA	Judy Schwomeyer James Sladky	Anne Millier Skip Millier	Mary Campbell Johnny Johns
1973 Minneapolis, MN	Mary Campbell Johnny Johns	Anne Millier Harvey Millier	Jane Pankey Richard Horne
1974 Providence, RI	Colleen O'Connor Jim Milins	Anne Millier Skip Millier	Michelle Ford Glenn Patterson
1975 Oakland, CA	Colleen O'Connor Jim Milins	Judi Genovesi Kent Weigle	Michelle Ford Glenn Patterson
1976 Colorado Springs, CO	Colleen O'Connor Jim Milins	Judi Genovesi Kent Weigle	Susan Kelley Andrew Stroukoff
1977 Hartford, CT	Judy Genovesi Kent Weigle	Susan Kelley Andrew Stroukoff	Michelle Ford Glenn Patterson
1978 Portland, OR	Stacey Smith John Summers	Carol Fox Richard Dalley	Susan Kelley Andrew Stroukoff
1979 Cincinnati, OH	Stacey Smith John Summers	Carol Fox Richard Dalley	Judy Blumberg Michael Seibert
1980 Atlanta, GA	Stacey Smith John Summers	Judy Blumberg Michael Seibert	Carol Fox Richard Dalley
1981 San Diego, CA	Judy Blumberg Michael Seibert	Carol Fox Richard Dalley	Kim Krohn Barry Hagan
1982 Indianapolis, IN	Judy Blumberg Michael Seibert	Carol Fox Richard Dalley	Elisa Spitz Scott Gregory
1983 Pittsburg, PA	Judy Blumberg Michael Seibert	Elisa Spitz Scott Gregory	Carol Fox Richard Dalley
1984 Salt Lake City, UT	Judy Blumberg Michael Seibert	Carol Fox Richard Dalley	Elisa Spitz Scott Gregory
1985 Kansas City, MO	Judy Blumberg Michael Seibert	Renee Roca Donald Adair	Suzanne Semanick Scott Gregory
1986 Long Island, NY	Renee Roca Donald Adair	Suzanne Semanick Scott Gregory	Lois Luciani Russ Witherby
1987 Tacoma, WA	Suzanne Semanick Scott Gregory	Renee Roca Donald Adair	Susan Wynne Joseph Druar
1988 Denver, CO	Suzanne Semanick Scott Gregory	Susan Wynne Joseph Druar	April Sargent Russ Witherby

	GOLD	SILVER	BRONZE
1989 Baltimore, MD	Susan Wynne Joseph Druar	April Sargent Russ Witherby	Suzanne Semanick Ron Kravette
1990 Salt Lake City, UT	Susan Wynne Joseph Druar	April Sargent Russ Witherby	Suzanne Semanick Ron Kravette
1991 Minneapolis, MN	Elizabeth Punsalan Jerod Swallow	April Sargent Russ Witherby	Jeanne Miley Michael Verlich
1992 Orlando, FL	April Sargent Russ Witherby	Rachel Mayer Peter Breen	Elizabeth Punsalan Jerod Swallow
1993 Phoenix, AZ	Renee Roca Gorsha Sur	Susan Wynne Russ Witherby	Elizabeth Punsalan Jerod Swallow

UNITED STATES
FIGURE SKATING CHAMPIONSHIPS

FOURS

	GOLD	SILVER	BRONZE
1924 Philadelphia, PA	Clara Hartman Grace Munstock Paul Armitage Joel Liberman	G. Pancoast Mrs. Joseph Chapman Joseph Chapman Charles Meyers	— — — —
1925 New York, NY	Clara Hartman Grace Munstock Paul Armitage Joel Liberman	— — — —	— — — —
1926–1933	**No Competition Held**		
1934 Philadelphia, PA	Suzanne Davis Theresa Weld Blanchard Frederick Goodridge Richard Hapgood	Valerie Jones Nettie Prantel Roy Hunt Joseph Savage	Hulda Berger E. Harris Arthur Janson Roland Janson
1935 New Haven, CT	Nettie Prantell Ardelle Kloss Joseph Savage Roy Hunt	Suzanne Davis Grace Madden George Hill Frederick Goodridge	Mrs. Banks Mrs. English W. R. Cady Len Fogassey
1936–38	**No Competition Held**		

	GOLD	SILVER	BRONZE
1939	Nettie Prantell	Mary Dayton	
St. Paul, MN	Marjorie Parker	Annah M. Hall	—
	Joseph Savage	William Hall	—
	George Boltres	William W. Lukens, Jr.	—
1940	Jannette Ahrens	Mary Stuart	—
Cleveland, OH	Mary Louise Premer	Dalton	—
		Annah M. Hall	—
	Robert Uppgren	William W.	—
	Lyman Wakefield Jr.	Lukens Jr. William Hall	
1941–1944	**No Competition Held**		
1945	Jacqueline Dunne	Jane Lemmon	Mary Anderson
New York, NY	Joan Yocum	Nancy Lemmon	Patricia Ryan
	Edward Van Der Bosch	Edgar Black	Henry Trenkamp
	Larry Van Der Bosch	Charles Brinkman	Gary Wilson
1946	Jacqueline Dunne	Sandra Rollinger	—
Chicago, IL	Joan Yocum	Nancy S. Jenkins	—
	Edward Van Der Bosch	Hayes Alan Jenkins	—
	Larry Van Der Bosch	Gary Wilson	—
1947	Janet Gerhauser	Joan Swanston	
Berkeley, CA	Marilyn Thomsen	Barbara Terrano	
	Marlyn Thomsen	Herman Maricich	
	John Nightingale	Robert O'Connell	
1948	Janet Gerhauser	Ferne Fletcher	Kathryn Ehlers
Colorado Springs, CO	Marilyn Thomsen	Anne Davis	Anne Hall
	Marlyn Thomsen	Carleton C. Hoffner	James Phillips
	John Nightingale	Donald Laws	Jean P. Brunet
1949	**No Competition Held**		
1950	Janet Gerhauser	Dorothy Dort	Barbara Davis
Washington, D.C.	Marilyn Thomsen	Mary Lou King	Elizabeth Jones
	Marlyn Thomsen	Daniel Ryan	William Lemmon
	John Nightingale	Richard Juten	James Coote
1951–1990	**No Competition Held**		
1991	Elaine Assanakis	Janis Bosch	—
Minneapolis, MN	Calla Urbanski	Laura LaBarca	—
	Joel McKeever	Kenneth Benson	—
	Rocky Marval	Sean Gales	—
1992	**No Competition Held**		
1993	**No Competition Held**		

WORLD CHAMPIONSHIPS

MEN'S SINGLES

	GOLD	SILVER	BRONZE
1896 St. Petersburg, RUS	Gilbert Fuchs (GER)	Gustav Hugel (AUT)	Georg Sanders (RUS)
1897 Stockholm, SWE	Gustav Hugel (AUT)	Ulrich Salchow (SWE)	Johan Lefstad (NOR)
1898 London, GBR	Henning Grenander (SWE)	Gustav Hugel (AUT)	Gilbert Fuchs (GER)
1899 Davos, SUI	Gustav Hugel (AUT)	Ulrich Salchow (SWE)	Edgar Syers (GBR)
1900 Davos, SUI	Gustav Hugel (AUT)	Ulrich Salchow (SWE)	—
1901 Stockholm, SWE	Ulrich Salchow (SWE)	Gilbert Fuchs (GER)	—
1902 London, GBR	Ulrich Salchow (SWE)	Madge Syers* (GBR)	Martin Gordan (GER)

*1902 marked the first year a woman applied to compete in the World Championships. At that time there was no provision in the rules for such an occurrence and it was not until 1903 that the congress decided that Ladies should not be permitted to compete at international men's championships. The Ladies event was introduced at the 1906 World Championships.

1903 St. Petersburg, RUS	Ulrich Salchow (SWE)	Nicolai Panin (RUS)	Max Bohatsch (AUT)
1904 Berlin, GER	Ulrich Salchow (SWE)	Heinrich Burger (GER)	Martin Gordan (GER)
1905 Stockholm, SWE	Ulrich Salchow (SWE)	Max Bohatsch (AUT)	Per Thoren (SWE)
1906 Munich, GER	Gilbert Fuchs (GER)	Heinrich Burger (GER)	Bror Meyer (SWE)
1907 Vienna, AUT	Ulrich Salchow (SWE)	Max Bohatsch (AUT)	Gilbert Fuchs (GER)
1908 Troppau, CZE	Ulrich Salchow (SWE)	Gilbert Fuchs (GER)	Heinrich Burger (GER)
1909 Stockholm, SWE	Ulrich Salchow (SWE)	Per Thoren (SWE)	Ernest Herz (AUT)
1910 Davos, SUI	Ulrich Salchow (SWE)	Werner Rittberger (GER)	Andor Szende (HUN)
1911 Berlin, GER	Ulrich Salchow (SWE)	Werner Rittberger (GER)	Fritz Kachler (AUT)

	GOLD	SILVER	BRONZE
1912 Manchester, GBR	Fritz Kachler (AUT)	Werner Rittberger (GER)	Andor Szende (HUN)
1913 Vienna, AUT	Fritz Kachler (AUT)	Willy Boeckl (AUT)	Andor Szende (HUN)
1914 Helsinki, FIN	Gosta Sandahl (SWE)	Fritz Kachler (AUT)	Willy Boeckl (AUT)
1915–1921	**No Championship Held**		
1922 Stockholm, SWE	Gillis Grafstrom (SWE)	Fritz Kachler (AUT)	Willy Boeckl (AUT)
1923 Vienna, AUT	Fritz Kachler (AUT)	Willy Boeckl (AUT)	Gosta Sandahl (SWE)
1924 Manchester, GBR	Gillis Grafstrom (SWE)	Willy Boeckl (AUT)	Ernst Oppacher (AUT)
1925 Vienna, AUT	Willy Boeckl (AUT)	Fritz Kachler (AUT)	Otto Preissecker (AUT)
1926 Berlin, GER	Willy Boeckl (AUT)	Otto Preissecker (AUT)	John Page (GBR)
1927 Davos, SUI	Willy Boeckl (AUT)	Otto Preissecker (AUT)	Karl Schafer (AUT)
1928 Berlin, GER	Willy Boeckl (AUT)	Karl Schafer (AUT)	Hugo Distler (AUT)
1929 London, GBR	Gillis Grafstrom (SWE)	Karl Schafer (AUT)	Ludwig Wrede (AUT)
1930 New York, USA	Karl Schafer (AUT)	Roger Turner (USA)	Georg Gautschi (SUI)
1931 Berlin, GER	Karl Schafer (AUT)	Roger Turner (USA)	Ernst Baier (GER)
1932 Montreal, CAN	Karl Schafer (AUT)	Montgomery Wilson (CAN)	Ernst Baier (GER)
1933 Zurich, SUI	Karl Schafer (AUT)	Ernst Baier (GER)	Markus Nikkanen (FIN)
1934 Stockholm, SWE	Karl Schafer (AUT)	Ernst Baier (GER)	Erich Erdos (AUT)
1935 Budapest, HUN	Karl Schafer (AUT)	Jack Dunn (GBR)	Denes Pataky (HUN)
1936 Paris, FRA	Karl Schafer (AUT)	Graham Sharp (GBR)	Felix Kaspar (AUT)
1937 Vienna, AUT	Felix Kaspar (AUT)	Graham Sharp (GBR)	Elemer Tertak (HUN)
1938 Berlin, GER	Felix Kaspar (AUT)	Graham Sharp (GBR)	Herbert Alward (AUT)

	GOLD	SILVER	BRONZE
1939 Budapest, HUN	Graham Sharp (GBR)	Freddie Tomlins (GBR)	Horst Faber (GER)
1940–1946	**No Championship Held**		
1947 Stockholm, SWE	Hans Gerschwiler (SUI)	Richard Button (USA)	Arthur Apfel (GBR)
1948 Davos, SUI	Richard Button (USA)	Hans Gerschwiler (SUI)	Ede Kiraly (HUN)
1949 Paris, FRA	Richard Button (USA)	Ede Kiraly (HUN)	Edi Rada (AUT)
1950 London, GBR	Richard Button (USA)	Ede Kiraly (HUN)	Hayes Jenkins (USA)
1951 Milan, ITA	Richard Button (USA)	James Grogan (USA)	Helmut Seibt (AUT)
1952 Paris, FRA	Richard Button (USA)	James Grogan (USA)	Hayes Jenkins (USA)
1953 Davos, SUI	Hayes Jenkins (USA)	James Grogan (USA)	Carlo Fassi (ITA)
1954 Oslo, NOR	Hayes Jenkins (USA)	James Grogan (USA)	Alain Giletti (FRA)
1955 Vienna, AUT	Hayes Jenkins (USA)	Ronald Robertson (USA)	David Jenkins (USA)
1956 Garmisch, FRG	Hayes Jenkins (USA)	Ronald Roberston (USA)	David Jenkins (USA)
1957 Colo. Spgs., USA	David Jenkins (USA)	Tim Brown (USA)	Charles Snelling (CAN)
1958 Paris, FRA	David Jenkins (USA)	Tim Brown (USA)	Alain Giletti (FRA)
1959 Colo. Spgs., USA	David Jenkins (USA)	Donald Jackson (CAN)	Tim Brown (USA)
1960 Vancouver, CAN	Alain Gilletti (FRA)	Donald Jackson (CAN)	Alain Calmat (FRA)
1961	**No Championship Held**		
1962 Prague, CZE	Donald Jackson (CAN)	Karol Divin (CZE)	Alain Calmat (FRA)
1963 Cortina, ITA	Donald McPherson (CAN)	Alain Calmat (FRA)	Manfred Schnelldorfer (FRG)
1964 Dortmund, FRG	Manfred Schnelldorfer (FRG)	Alain Calmat (FRA)	Karol Divin (CZE)
1965 Colo. Spgs., USA	Alain Calmat (FRA)	Scott Allen (USA)	Donald Knight (CAN)

	GOLD	SILVER	BRONZE
1966 Davos, SUI	Emmerich Danzer (AUT)	Wolfgang Schwarz (AUT)	Gary Visconti (USA)
1967 Vienna, AUT	Emmerich Danzer (AUT)	Wolfgang Schwarz (AUT)	Gary Visconti (USA)
1968 Geneva, SUI	Emmerich Danzer (AUT)	Tim Wood (USA)	Patrick Pera (FRA)
1969 Colo. Spgs., USA	Tim Wood (USA)	Ondrej Nepela (CZE)	Patrick Pera (FRA)
1970 Ljubljana, YUG	Tim Wood (USA)	Ondrej Nepela (CZE)	Gunter Zoller (GDR)
1971 Lyon, FRA	Ondrej Nepela (CZE)	Patrick Pera (FRA)	Sergei Chetverukhin (URS)
1972 Calgary, CAN	Ondrej Nepela (CZE)	Sergei Chetverukhin (URS)	Vladimir Kovalev (URS)
1973 Bratslava, CZE	Ondrej Nepela (CZE)	Sergei Chetverukhin (URS)	Jan Hoffmann (GDR)
1974 Munich, FRG	Jan Hoffmann (GDR)	Sergei Volkov (URS)	Toller Cranston (CAN)
1975 Colo. Spgs., USA	Sergei Volkov (URS)	Vladimir Kovalev (URS)	John Curry (GBR)
1976 Gothenberg, SWE	John Curry (GBR)	Vladimir Kovalev (URS)	Jan Hoffmann (GDR)
1977 Tokyo, JPN	Vladimir Kovalev (URS)	Jan Hoffmann (GDR)	Minoru Sano (JPN)
1978 Ottawa, CAN	Charles Tickner (USA)	Jan Hoffmann (GDR)	Robin Cousins (GBR)
1979 Vienna, AUT	Vladimir Kovalev (URS)	Robin Cousins (GBR)	Jan Hoffmann (GDR)
1980 Dortmund, FRG	Jan Hoffmann (GDR)	Robin Cousins (GBR)	Charles Tickner (USA)
1981 Hartford, USA	Scott Hamilton (USA)	David Santee (USA)	Igor Bobrin (URS)
1982 Copenhagen, DEN	Scott Hamilton (USA)	Norbert Schramm (FRG)	Brian Pockar (CAN)
1983 Helsinki, FIN	Scott Hamilton (USA)	Norbert Schramm (FRG)	Brian Orser (CAN)
1984 Ottawa, CAN	Scott Hamilton (USA)	Brian Orser (CAN)	Alexandr Fadeev (URS)

	GOLD	SILVER	BRONZE
1985 Tokyo, JPN	Alexandr Fadeev (URS)	Brian Orser (CAN)	Brian Boitano (USA)
1986 Geneva, SUI	Brian Boitano (USA)	Brian Orser (CAN)	Alexandr Fadeev (URS)
1987 Cincinnati, USA	Brian Orser (CAN)	Brian Boitano (USA)	Alexandr Fadeev (URS)
1988 Budapest, HUN	Brian Boitano (USA)	Brian Orser (CAN)	Viktor Petrenko (URS)
1989 Paris, FRA	Kurt Browning (CAN)	Christopher Bowman (USA)	Grzegorz Filipowski (POL)
1990 Halifax, CAN	Kurt Browning (CAN)	Viktor Petrenko (URS)	Christopher Bowman (USA)
1991 Munich, GER	Kurt Browning (CAN)	Viktor Petrenko (URS)	Todd Eldredge (USA)
1992 Oakland, USA	Viktor Petrenko (CIS)	Kurt Browning (CAN)	Elvis Stojko (CAN)
1993 Prague, Czech Rep.	Kurt Browning (CAN)	Elvis Stojko (CAN)	Alexei Urmanov (RUS)

WORLD CHAMPIONSHIPS

LADIES' SINGLES

	GOLD	SILVER	BRONZE
1906 Davos, SUI	Madge Syers (GBR)	Jenny Herz (AUT)	Lily Kronberger (HUN)
1907 Vienna, AUS	Madge Syers (GBR)	Jenny Herz (AUT)	Lily Kronberger (HUN)
1908 Troppau, CZE	Lily Kronberger (HUN)	Elsa Rendschmidt (GER)	—
1909 Budapest, HUN	Lily Kronberger (HUN)	—	—
1910 Berlin, GER	Lily Kronberger (HUN)	Elsa Rendschmidt (GER)	—
1911 Vienna, AUT	Lily Kronberger (HUN)	Opika von Horvath (HUN)	Ludowika Eilers (GER)
1912 Davos, SUI	Opika von Horvath (HUN)	Dorothy Greenhough (GBR)	Phyllis Johnson (GBR)

	GOLD	SILVER	BRONZE
1913 Stockholm, SWE	Opika von Horvath (HUN)	Phyllis Johnson (GBR)	Svea Noren (SWE)
1914 St. Moritz, SUI	Opika von Horvath (HUN)	Angela Hanka (AUT)	Phyllis Johnson (GBR)
1915–1921	**No Championship Held**		
1922 Stockholm, SWE	Herma Plank- Szabo (AUT)	Svea Noren (SWE)	Margot Moe (NOR)
1923 Vienna, AUT	Herma Plank- Szabo (AUT)	Gisela Reichmann (AUT)	Svea Noren (SWE)
1924 Oslo, NOR	Herma Plank- Szabo (AUT)	Ellen Brockhofft (GER)	Beatrix Loughran (USA)
1925 Davos, SUI	Herma Jaross- Szabo (AUT)	Ellen Brockhofft (GER)	Elisabeth Bockel (GER)
1926 Stockholm, SWE	Herma Jaross- Szabo (AUT)	Sonja Henie (NOR)	Kathleen Shaw (GBR)
1927 Oslo, NOR	Sonja Henie (NOR)	Herma Jaross- Szabo (AUT)	Karen Simensen (NOR)
1928 London, GBR	Sonja Henie (NOR)	Maribel Vinson (USA)	Fritzi Burger (AUT)
1929 Budapest, HUN	Sonja Henie (NOR)	Fritzi Burger (AUT)	Melitta Brunner (AUT)
1930 New York, USA	Sonja Henie (NOR)	Cecil Smith (CAN)	Maribel Vinson (USA)
1931 Berlin, GER	Sonja Henie (NOR)	Hilde Holovsky (AUT)	Fritzi Burger (AUT)
1932 Montreal, CAN	Sonja Henie (NOR)	Fritzi Burger (AUT)	Constance Samuel (CAN)
1933 Stockholm, SWE	Sonja Henie (NOR)	Vivi-Anne Hulten (SWE)	Hilde Holovsky (AUT)
1934 Oslo, NOR	Sonja Henie (NOR)	Megan Taylor (GBR)	Liselotte Landbeck (AUT)
1935 Vienna, AUT	Sonja Henie (NOR)	Cecilia Colledge (GBR)	Vivi-Anne Hulten (SWE)
1936 Paris, FRA	Sonja Henie (NOR)	Megan Taylor (GBR)	Vivi-Anne Hulten (SWE)

	GOLD	SILVER	BRONZE
1937 London, GBR	Cecilia Colledge (GBR)	Megan Taylor (GBR)	Vivi-Anne Hulten (SWE)
1938 Stockholm, SWE	Megan Taylor (GBR)	Cecilia Colledge (GBR)	Hedy Stenuf (USA)
1939 Prague, CZE	Megan Taylor (GBR)	Hedy Stenuf (USA)	Daphne Walker (GBR)
1940–1946	**No Championship Held**		
1947 Stockholm, SWE	Barbara Ann Scott (CAN)	Daphne Walker (GBR)	Gretchen Merrill (USA)
1948 Davos, SUI	Barbara Ann Scott (CAN)	Eva Pawlik (AUT)	Jirina Nekolova (CZE)
1949 Paris, FRA	Alena Vrzanova (CZE)	Yvonne Sherman (USA)	Jeannette Altwegg (GBR)
1950 London, GBR	Alena Vrzanova (CZE)	Jeannette Altwegg (GBR)	Yvonne Sherman (USA)
1951 Milan, ITA	Jeannette Altwegg (GBR)	Jacqueline du Bief (FRA)	Sonya Klopfer (USA)
1952 Paris, FRA	Jacqueline de Bief (FRA)	Sonja Klopfer (USA)	Virginia Baxter (USA)
1953 Davos, SUI	Tenley Albright (USA)	Gundi Busch (FRG)	Valda Osborn (GBR)
1954 Oslo, NOR	Gundi Busch (FRG)	Tenley Albright (USA)	Erica Batchelor (GBR)
1955 Vienna, AUT	Tenley Albright (USA)	Carol Heiss (USA)	Hanna Eigel (AUT)
1956 Garmisch, FRG	Carol Heiss (USA)	Tenley Albright (USA)	Ingrid Wendl (AUT)
1957 Colo. Spgs., USA	Carol Heiss (USA)	Hanna Eigel (AUT)	Ingrid Wendl (AUT)
1958 Paris, FRA	Carol Heiss (USA)	Ingrid Wendl (AUT)	Hanna Walter (AUT)
1959 Colo. Spgs., USA	Carol Heiss (USA)	Hanna Walter (AUT)	Sjoukje Dijkstra (HOL)
1960 Vancouver, CAN	Carol Heiss (USA)	Sjoukje Dijkstra (HOL)	Barbara Roles (USA)
1961	**No Championship Held**		
1962 Prague, CZE	Sjoukje Dijkstra (HOL)	Wendy Griner (CAN)	Regine Heitzer (AUT)
1963 Cortina, ITA	Sjoukje Dijkstra (HOL)	Regine Heitzer (AUT)	Nicole Hassler (FRA)
1964 Dortmund, FRG	Sjouke Dijkstra (HOL)	Regine Heitzer (AUT)	Petra Burks (CAN)

	GOLD	SILVER	BRONZE
1965 Colo. Spgs., USA	Petra Burka (CAN)	Regine Heitzer (AUT)	Peggy Fleming (USA)
1966 Davos, SUI	Peggy Fleming (USA)	Gabriele Seyfert (GDR)	Petra Burka (CAN)
1967 Vienna, AUT	Peggy Fleming (USA)	Gabriele Seyfert (GDR)	Hana Maskova (CZE)
1968 Geneva, SUI	Peggy Fleming (USA)	Gabriele Seyfert (GDR)	Hana Maskova (CZE)
1969 Colo. Spgs., USA	Gabriele Seyfert (GDR)	Beatrix Schuba (AUT)	Zsuzsa Almassy (HUN)
1970 Ljubljana, YUG	Gabriele Seyfert (GDR)	Beatrix Schuba (AUT)	Julie Holmes (USA)
1971 Lyon, FRA	Beatrix Schuba (AUT)	Julie Holmes (USA)	Karen Magnussen (CAN)
1972 Calgary, CAN	Beatrix Schuba (AUT)	Karen Magnussen (CAN)	Janet Lynn (USA)
1973 Bratislava, CZE	Karen Magnussen (CAN)	Janet Lynn (USA)	Christine Errath (GDR)
1974 Munich, FRG	Christine Errath (GDR)	Dorothy Hamill (USA)	Dianne de Leeuw (HOL)
1975 Colo. Spgs., USA	Dianne de Leeuw (HOL)	Dorothy Hamill (USA)	Christine Errath (GDR)
1976 Gothenberg, SWE	Dorothy Hamill (USA)	Christine Errath (GDR)	Dianne de Leeuw (HOL)
1977 Tokyo, JPN	Linda Fratianne (USA)	Anett Poetzsch (GDR)	Dagmar Lurz (FRG)
1978 Ottawa, CAN	Anett Poetzsch (GDR)	Linda Fratianne (USA)	Susanna Driano (ITA)
1979 Vienna, AUT	Linda Fratianne (USA)	Anett Poetzsch (GDR)	Emi Watanabe (JPN)
1980 Dortmund, FRG	Anett Poetzsch (GDR)	Dagmar Lurz (FRG)	Linda Fratianne (USA)
1981 Hartford, USA	Denise Biellmann (SUI)	Elaine Zayak (USA)	Claudia Kristofics- Binder (AUT)
1982 Copenhagen, DEN	Elaine Zayak (USA)	Katarina Witt (GDR)	Claudia Kristofics- Binder (AUT)
1983 Helsinki, FIN	Rosalynn Sumners (USA)	Claudia Leistner (FRG)	Elena Vodorezova (URS)
1984 Ottawa, CAN	Katarina Witt (GDR)	Anna Kondrashova (URS)	Elaine Zayak (USA)

	GOLD	SILVER	BRONZE
1985 Tokyo, JPN	Katarina Witt (GDR)	Kira Ivanova (URS)	Tiffany Chin (USA)
1986 Geneva, SUI	Debi Thomas (USA)	Katarina Witt (GDR)	Tiffany Chin (USA)
1987 Cincinnati, USA	Katarina Witt (GDR)	Debi Thomas (USA)	Caryn Kadavy (USA)
1988 Budapest, HUN	Katarina Witt (GDR)	Elizabeth Manley (CAN)	Debi Thomas (USA)
1989 Paris, FRA	Midori Ito (JPN)	Claudia Leistner (FRG)	Jill Trenary (USA)
1990 Halifax, CAN	Jill Trenary (USA)	Midori Ito (JPN)	Holly Cook (USA)
1991 Munich, GER	Kristi Yamaguchi (USA)	Tonya Harding (USA)	Nancy Kerrigan (USA)
1992 Oakland, USA	Kristi Yamaguchi (USA)	Nancy Kerrigan (USA)	Lu Chen (CHN)
1993 Prague, Czech Rep.	Oksana Baiul (UKR)	Surya Bonaly (FRA)	Lu Chen (CHN)

WORLD CHAMPIONSHIPS

PAIRS

	GOLD	SILVER	BRONZE
1908 St. Petersburg, RUS	Anna Hubler Heinrich Burger (GER)	Phyllis Johnson James Johnson (GBR)	A. Fischer L. Popowa (RUS)
1909 Stockholm, SWE	Phyllis Johnson James Johnson (GBR)	Valborg Lindahl Nils Rosenius (SWE)	Gertrud Strom Richard Johanson (SWE)
1910 Berlin, GER	Anna Hubler Henrich Burger (GER)	Ludowika Eilers Walter Jakobsson (FIN)	Phyllis Johnson James Johnson (GBR)
1911 Vienna, AUT	Ludowika Eilers Walter Jakobsson (FIN)	—	—
1912 Manchester, GBR	Phyllis Johnson James Johnson (GBR)	Ludowika Jakobsson Walter Jakobsson (FIN)	Alexia Schoyen Yngvar Bryn (NOR)

	GOLD	SILVER	BRONZE
1913 Stockholm, SWE	Helene Engelmann Karl Mejstrik (AUT)	Ludowika Jakobsson Walter Jakobsson (FIN)	Christa von Szabo Leo Horwitz (AUT)
1914 St. Moritz, SUI	Ludowika Jakobsson Walter Jakobsson (FIN)	Helene Engelmann Karl Maejstrik (AUT)	Christa von Szabo Leo Horwitz (AUT)
1915–1921	**No Championship Held**		
1922 Davos, SUI	Helene Engelmann Alfred Berger (AUT)	Ludowika Jakobbson Walter Jakobbson (FIN)	Margaret Metzner Paul Metzner (GER)
1923 Oslo, NOR	Ludowika Jakobsson Walter Jakobsson (FIN)	Alexia Bryn Yngvar Bryn (NOR)	Elna Henrikson Kaj af Ekstrom (SWE)
1924 Manchester, GBR	Helene Engelmann Alfred Berger (AUT)	Ethel Muckelt John Page (GBR)	Elna Henrikson Kajaf Ekstrom (SWE)
1925 Vienna, AUT	Herma Jaross- Szabo Ludwig Wrede (AUT)	Andree Brunet Pierre Brunet (FRA)	Lilly Scholz Otto Kaiser (AUT)
1926 Berlin, GER	Andree Brunet Pierre Brunet (FRA)	Lilly Scholz Otto Kaiser (AUT)	Herma Jaross- Szabo Ludwig Wrede (AUT)
1927 Vienna, AUT	Herma Jaross- Szabo Ludwig Wrede (AUT)	Lilly Scholz Otto Kaiser (AUT)	Else Hoppe Oscar Hoppe (CZE)
1928 London, GBR	Andree Brunet Pierre Brunet (FRA)	Lilly Scholz Otto Kaiser (AUT)	Melitta Brunner Ludwig Wrede (AUT)
1929 Budapest, HUN	Lilly Scholz Otto Kaiser (AUT)	Melitta Brunner Ludwig Wrede (AUT)	Olga Orgonista Sandor Szalay (HUN)
1930 New York, USA	Andree Brunet Pierre Brunet (FRA)	Melitta Brunner Ludwig Wrede (AUT)	Beatrix Loughran Sherwin Badger (USA)
1931 Berlin, GER	Emilie Rotter Laszlo Szollas (HUN)	Olga Orgonista Sandor Szalay (HUN)	Idi Papez Karl Kwack (AUT)

	GOLD	SILVER	BRONZE
1932 Montreal, CAN	Andree Brunet Pierre Brunet (FRA)	Emilie Rotter Laszlo Szollas (HUN)	Beatrix Loughran Sherwin Badger (USA)
1933 Stockholm, SWE	Emilie Rotter Laszlo Szollas (HUN)	Idi Papez Karl Zwack (AUT)	Randi Bakke Christen Christensen (NOR)
1934 Helsinki, FIN	Emilie Rotter Laszlo Szollas (HUN)	Idi Papez Karl Zwack (AUT)	Maxi Herber Ernst Baier (GER)
1935 Budapest, HUN	Emilie Rotter Laszlo Szollas (HUN)	Ilse Pausin Erich Pausin (AUT)	Lucy Gallo Rezso Dillinger (HUN)
1936 Paris, FRA	Maxi Herber Ernst Baier (GER)	Ilse Pausin Erich Pausin (AUT)	Violet Cliff Leslie Cliff (GBR)
1937 London, GBR	Maxi Herber Ernst Baier (GER)	Ilse Pausin Erich Pausin (AUT)	Violet Cliff Leslie Cliff (GBR)
1938 Berlin, GER	Maxi Herber Ernst Baier (GER)	Ilse Pausin Erich Pausin (AUT)	Inge Koch Gunther Noack (GER)
1939 Budapest, HUN	Maxi Herber Ernst Baier (GER)	Ilse Pausin Erich Pausin (AUT)	Inge Koch Gunther Koack (GER)
1940–1946	**No Championship Held**		
1947 Stockholm, SWE	Micheline Lannoy Pierre Baugniet (BEL)	Karol Kennedy Peter Kennedy (USA)	Suzanne Diskeuve Edmond Verbustel (BEL)
1948 Davos, SUI	Micheline Lannoy Pierre Baugniet (BEL)	Andrea Kekesy Ede Kiraly (HUN)	Suzanne Morrow Wallace Diestelmeyer (CAN)
1949 Paris, FRA	Andrea Kekesy Ede Kiraly (HUN)	Karol Kennedy Peter Kennedy (USA)	Anne Davies Carleton Hoffner (USA)
1950 London, GBR	Karol Kennedy Peter Kennedy (USA)	Jennifer Nicks John Nicks (GBR)	Marianne Nagy Laszlo Nagy (HUN)
1951 Milan, ITA	Ria Falk Paul Falk (FRG)	Karol Kennedy Peter Kennedy (USA)	Jennifer Nicks John Nicks (GBR)
1952 Paris, FRA	Ria Falk Paul Falk (FRG)	Karol Kennedy Peter Kennedy (USA)	Jennifer Nicks John Nicks (GBR)

	GOLD	SILVER	BRONZE
1953 Davos, SUI	Jennifer Nicks John Nicks (GBR)	Frances Dafoe Norris Bowden (CAN)	Marianne Nagy Laszlo Nagy (HUN)
1954 Oslo, NOR	Frances Dafoe Norris Bowden (CAN)	Silvia Grandjean Michel Grandjean (SUI)	Elisabeth Schwarz Kurt Oppelt (AUT)
1955 Vienna, AUT	Frances Dafoe Norris Bowden (CAN)	Elisabeth Schwarz Kurt Oppelt (AUT)	Marianne Nagy Laszlo Nagy (HUN)
1956 Garmisch, FRG	Elisabeth Schwarz Kurt Oppelt (AUT)	Frances Dafoe Norris Bowden (CAN)	Marika Kilius Franz Ningel (FRG)
1957 Colo. Spgs., USA	Barbara Wagner Robert Paul (CAN)	Marika Kilius Franz Ningel (FRG)	Maria Jelinek Otto Jelinek (CAN)
1958 Paris, FRA	Barbara Wagner Robert Paul (CAN)	Vera Suchankova Zdenek Dolezal (CZE)	Maria Jelinek Otto Jelinek (CAN)
1959 Colo. Spgs., USA	Barbara Wagner Robert Paul (CAN)	Marika Kilius Hans Baumler (FRG)	Nancy Ludington Ronald Ludington (USA)
1960 Vancouver, CAN	Barbara Wagner Robert Paul (CAN)	Maria Jelinek Otto Jelinek (CAN)	Marika Kilius Hans Baumler (FRG)
1961	**No Championship Held**		
1962 Prague, CZE	Maria Jelinek Otto Jelinek (CAN)	Ludmila Belousova Oleg Protopopov (URS)	Margret Gobl Franz Ningel (FRG)
1963 Cortina, ITA	Marika Kilius Hans Baumler (FRG)	Ludmila Belousova Oleg Protopopov (URS)	Tatiana Zhuk Alexandr Gavrilov (URS)
1964 Dortmund, FRG	Marika Kilius Hans Baumler (FRG)	Ludmila Belousova Oleg Protopopov (URS)	Debbi Wilkes Guy Revell (CAN)
1965 Colo. Spgs., USA	Ludmila Belousova Oleg Protopopov (URS)	Vivian Joseph Ronald Joseph (USA)	Tatiana Zhuk Alexandr Gorelik (URS)
1966 Davos, SUI	Ludmila Belousova Oleg Protopopov (URS)	Tatiana Zhuk Alexandr Gorelik (URS)	Cynthia Kauffman Ronald Kauffman (USA)

	GOLD	SILVER	BRONZE
1967 Vienna, AUT	Ludmila Belousova Oleg Protopopov (URS)	Margot Glockshuber Wolfgang Danne (FRG)	Cynthia Kauffman Ronald Kauffman (USA)
1968 Geneva, SUI	Ludmila Belousova Oleg Protopopov (URS)	Tatiana Zhuk Alexandr Gorelik (URS)	Cynthia Kauffman Ronald Kauffman (USA)
1969 Colo. Spgs., USA	Irina Rodnina Alexsei Ulanov (URS)	Tamara Moskvina Alexsel Mishin (URS)	Ludmila Belousova Oleg Protopopov (URS)
1970 Ljubljana, YUG	Irina Rodnina Alexsel Ulanov (URS)	Ludmila Smmirnova Andrei Suraikin (URS)	Heidemarie Steiner Heinz Walther (GDR)
1971 Lyon, FRA	Irina Rodnina Alexsel Ulanov (URS)	Ludmila Smirnova Andrei Suraikin (URS)	JoJo Starbuck Kenneth Shelley (USA)
1972 Calgary, CAN	Irina Rodnina Alexsei Ulanov (URS)	Ludmila Smirnova Andrei Suraikin (URS)	JoJo Starbuck Kenneth Shelley (USA)
1973 Bratislava, CZE	Irina Rodnina Alexandr Zaitsev (URS)	Ludmila Smirnova Alexsei Ulanov (URS)	Manuela Gross Uwe Kagelmann (GDR)
1974 Munich, FRG	Irina Rodnina Alexandr Zaltsev (URS)	Ludmila Smirnova Alexsei Ulanov (URS)	Romy Kermer Rolf Osterreich (GDR)
1975 Colo. Spgs., USA	Irina Rodnina Alexandr Zaitsev (URS)	Romy Kermer Rolf Osterreich (GDR)	Manuela Gross Uwe Kagelmann (GDR)
1976 Gothenberg, SWE	Irina Rodnina Alexandr Zaitsev (URS)	Romy Kermer Rolf Osterreich (GDR)	Irina Vorobieva Alexandr Vlasov (URS)
1977 Tokyo, JPN	Irina Rodnina Alexandr Zaitsev (URS)	Irina Vorobieva Alexandr Vlasov (URS)	Tai Babilonia Randy Gardner (USA)
1978 Ottawa, CAN	Irina Rodnina Alexandr Zaitsev (URS)	Manuela Mager Uwe Bewersdorff (GDR)	Tai Babilonia Randy Gardner (USA)
1979 Vienna, AUT	Tai Babilonia Randy Gardner (USA)	Marina Cherkosova Sergei Shakhrai (URS)	Sabine Baess Tassilo Theirbach (GDR)

	GOLD	SILVER	BRONZE
1980 Dortmund, FRG	Marina Cherkasova Sergei Shakhral (URS)	Manuela Mager Uwe Bewersdorf (GDR)	Marina Pestova Stanislav Leonovich (URS)
1981 Hartford, USA	Irina Vorobieva Igor Lisovsky (URS)	Sabine Baess Tassilo Thierbach (GDR)	Christina Riegel Andreas Nischwitz (FRG)
1982 Copenhagen, DEN	Sabine Baess Tassilo Thierbach (GDR)	Marina Pestova Stansilav Leonovich (URS)	Caitlin Carruthers Peter Carruthers (USA)
1983 Helsinki, FIN	Elena Valova Oleg Vasiliev (URS)	Sabine Baess Tassilo Thierbach (GDR)	Barbara Underhill Paul Martini (CAN)
1984 Ottawa, CAN	Barbara Underhill Paul Martini (CAN)	Elena Valova Oleg Vasiliev (URS)	Sabine Baess Tassilo Thierbach (GDR)
1985 Tokyo, JPN	Elena Valova Oleg Vasiliev (URS)	Larisa Selezneva Oleg Makarov (URS)	Katherina Matousek Lloyd Eisler (CAN)
1986 Geneva, SUI	Ekaterina Gordeeva Sergi Grinkov (URS)	Elena Valova Oleg Vasiliev (URS)	Cynthia Coull Mark Rowsom (CAN)
1987 Cincinnati, USA	Ekaterina Gordeeva Sergei Grinkov (URS)	Elena Valova Oleg Vasiliev (URS)	Jill Watson Peter Oppegard (USA)
1988 Budapest, HUN	Elena Valova Oleg Vasiliev (URS)	Ekaterina Gordeeva Sergei Grinkov (URS)	Larisa Selezneva Oleg Makarov (URS)
1989 Paris, FRA	Ekaterina Gordeeva Sergei Grinkov (URS)	Cindy Landry Lyndon Johnston (CAN)	Elena Bechke Denis Petrov (URS)
1990 Halifax, CAN	Ekaterina Gordeeva Sergei Grinkov (URS)	Isabelle Brasseur Lloyd Eisler (CAN)	Natalia Mishkutenok Artur Dmitriev (URS)
1991 Munich, GER	Natalia Mishkutenok Artur Dmitriev (URS)	Isabelle Brasseur Lloyd Eisler (CAN)	Natasha Kuchiki Todd Sand (USA)

	GOLD	SILVER	BRONZE
1992 Oakland, USA	Natalia Mishkutenok Artur Dmitriev (CIS)	Radka Kovarikova Rene Novotny (CIS)	Isabelle Brasseur Lloyd Eisler (CAN)
1993 Prague, Czech Rep.	Isabelle Brasseur Lloyd Eisler (CAN)	Mandy Wötzel Ingo Steuer (GER)	Evgenia Shishkova Vadim Naumov (RUS)

WORLD CHAMPIONSHIPS

ICE DANCING

	GOLD	SILVER	BRONZE
1952 Paris, FRA	Jean Westwood Lawrence Demmy (GBR)	Joan Dewhirst John Slater (GBR)	Carol Peters Daniel Ryan (USA)
1953 Davos, SUI	Jean Westwood Lawrence Demmy (GBR)	Joan Dewhirts John Slater (GBR)	Carol Peters Daniel Ryan (USA)
1954 Oslo, NOR	Jean Westwood Lawrence Demmy (GBR)	Nesta Davies Paul Thomas (GBR)	Carmel Bodel Edward Bodel (USA)
1955 Vienna, AUT	Jean Westwood Lawrence Demmy (GBR)	Pamela Weight Paul Thomas (GBR)	Barbara Radford Raymond Lockwood (GBR)
1956 Garmisch, FRG	Pamela Weight Paul Thomas (GBR)	June Markham Courtney Jones (GBR)	Barbara Thompson Gerard Rigby (GBR)
1957 Colo. Spgs., USA	June Markham Courtney Jones (GBR)	Geraldine Fenton William McLachian (CAN)	Sharon McKenzie Bert Wright (USA)
1958 Paris, FRA	June Markham Courtney Jones (GBR)	Geraldine Fenton William McLachian (CAN)	Andree Anderson Donald Jacoby (USA)
1959 Colo. Spgs., USA	Doreen Denny Courtney Jones (GBR)	Andree Anderson Donald Jacoby (USA)	Geraldine Fenton William McLachian (CAN)
1960 Vancouver, CAN	Doreen Denny Courtney Jones (GBR)	Virginia Thompson William McLachian (CAN)	Christine Guhel Jean Paul Guhel (FRA)

	GOLD	SILVER	BRONZE
1961	**No Competition Held**		
1962 Prague, CZE	Eva Romanova Pavel Roman (CZE)	Christine Guhel Jean Paul Guhel (FRA)	Virginia Thompson William McLachian (CAN)
1963 Cortina, ITA	Eva Romanova Pavel Roman (CZE)	Linda Shearman Michael Phillips (GBR)	Paulette Doan Kenneth Ormsby (CAN)
1964 Dortmund, FRG	Eva Romanova Pavel Roman (CZE)	Paulette Doan Kenneth Ormsby (CAN)	Janet Sawbridge David Hickinbottom (GBR)
1965 Colo. Spgs., USA	Eva Romanova Pavel Roman (CZE)	Janet Sawbridge David Hickinbottom (GBR)	Lorna Dyer John Carrell (USA)
1966 Davos, SUI	Diane Towler Bernard Ford (GBR)	Kristin Fortune Dennis Sveum (USA)	Lorna Dyer John Carrell (USA)
1967 Vienna, AUT	Diane Towler Bernard Ford (GBR)	Lorna Dyer John Carrell (USA)	Yvonne Suddick Malcolm Cannon (GBR)
1968 Geneva, SUI	Diane Towler Bernard Ford (GBR)	Yvonne Suddick Malcolm Cannon (GBR)	Janet Sawbridge Jon Lane (GBR)
1969 Colo. Spgs., USA	Diane Towler Bernard Ford (GBR)	Ludmila Pakhomova Aleksandr Gorshkov (URS)	Judy Schwomeyer James Sladky (USA)
1970 Ljubljana, YUG	Ludmila Pakhomova Aleksandr Gorshkov (URS)	Judy Schwomeyer James Sladky (USA)	Angelika Buck Erich Buck (FRG)
1971 Lyon, FRA	Ludmila Pakhomova Aleksandr Gorshkov (URS)	Angelika Buck Erich Buck (FRG)	Judy Schwomeyer James Sladky (USA)
1972 Calgary, CAN	Ludmila Pakhomova Aleksandr Gorschkov (URS)	Angelika Buck Erich Buck (FRG)	Judy Schwomeyer James Sladky (USA)

	GOLD	SILVER	BRONZE
1973 Bratislava, CZE	Ludmila Pakhomova Aleksandr Gorshkov (URS)	Angelika Buck Erich Buck (FRG)	Hilary Green Glyn Watts (GBR)
1974 Munich, FRG	Ludmila Pakhomova Aleksandr Gorshkov (URS)	Hilary Green Glyn Watts (GBR)	Natalia Linichuk Gennadi Karponosov (URS)
1975 Colo. Spgs., USA	Irina Molseeva Andrei Minenkov (URS)	Colleen O'Connor Jim Milins (USA)	Hilary Green Glyn Watts (GBR)
1976 Gothenberg, SWE	Ludmila Pakhomova Aleksandr Gorshkov (URS)	Irina Molseeva Andrei Minenkov (URS)	Colleen O'Connor Jim Milins (USA)
1977 Tokyo, JPN	Irina Molseeva Andrei Minenkov (URS)	Janet Thompson Warren Maxwell (GBR)	Natalia Linichuk Gennadi Karponosov (URS)
1978 Ottawa, CAN	Natalia Linichuk Gennadi Karponosov (URS)	Irina Molseeva Andrei Minenkov (URS)	Krisztina Regoeczy Andras Sallay (HUN)
1979 Vienna, AUT	Natalia Linichuk Gennadi Karponosov (URS)	Krisztina Regoeczy Andras Sallay (HUN)	Irina Molseeva Andrei Minenkov (URS)
1980 Dortmund, FRG	Krisztina Regoeczy Andras Sallay (HUN)	Natalia Linichuk Gennadi Karponosov (URS)	Irina Molseeva Andrei Minenkov (URS)
1981 Hartford, USA	Jayne Torvill Christopher Dean (GRB)	Irina Molsseeva Andrei Minenkov (URS)	Natalia Bestemianova Andrei Bukin (URS)
1982 Copenhagen, DEN	Jayne Torvill Christopher Dean (GBR)	Natalia Bestemianova Andrei Bukin (URS)	Irina Molseeva Andrei Minenkov (URS)
1983 Helsinki, FIN	Jayne Torvill Christopher Dean (GBR)	Natalia Bestimianova Andrei Bukin (URS)	Judy Blumberg Michael Seibert (USA)

	GOLD	SILVER	BRONZE
1984 Ottawa, CAN	Jayne Torvill Christopher Dean (GBR)	Natalia Bestimianova Andrei Bukin (URS)	Judy Blumberg Michael Seibert (USA)
1985 Tokyo, JPN	Natalia Bestemianova Andrei Bukin (URS)	Marina Klimova Sergei Ponomarenko (URS)	Judy Blumberg Michael Seibert (USA)
1986 Geneva, SUI	Natalia Bestemianova Andrei Bukin (URS)	Marina Klimova Sergei Ponomarenko (URS)	Tracy Wilson Robert McCall (CAN)
1987 Cincinnati, USA	Natalia Bestemianova Andrei Bukin (URS)	Marina Klimova Sergei Ponomarenko (URS)	Tracy Wilson Robert McCall (CAN)
1988 Budapest, HUN	Natalia Bestemianova Andrei Bukin (URS)	Marina Klimova Sergei Ponomarenko (URS)	Tracy Wilson Robert McCall (CAN)
1989 Paris, FRA	Marina Klimova Sergei Ponomarenko (URS)	Mala Usova Alexander Zhulin (URS)	Isabelle Duchesnay Paul Duchesnay (FRA)
1990 Halifax, CAN	Marina Klimova Sergei Ponomarenko (URS)	Isabelle Duchesnay Paul Duchesnay (FRA)	Mala Usova Alexander Zhulin (URS)
1991 Munich, GER	Isabelle Duchesnay Paul Duchesnay (FRA)	Marina Klimova Sergei Ponomarenko (URS)	Mala Usova Alexander Zhulin (URS)
1992 Oakland, USA	Marina Klimova Sergei Ponomarenko (CIS)	Mala Usova Alexander Zhulin (CIS)	Oksana Gritschuk Evgeni Platov (CIS)
1993 Prague, Czech Rep.	Mala Usova Alexandr Zhulin (RUS)	Oksana Gritschuk Evgeny Platov (RUS)	Anjelika Krylova Vladimir Fedorov (RUS)

OLYMPIC WINTER GAMES

MEN'S SINGLES

	GOLD	SILVER	BRONZE
1908 London, GBR	Ulrich Salchow (SWE)	Richard Johannson (SWE)	Per Thoren (SWE)

	GOLD	SILVER	BRONZE
1920 Antwerp, BEL	Gillis Grafstom (SWE)	Andreas Krogh (NOR)	Martin Silxrud (NOR)
1924 Chamonix, FRA	Gillis Grafstrom (SWE)	Willy Boeckl (AUT)	Georg Gautschi (SUI)
1928 St. Mortiz, SUI	Gillis Grafstrom (SWE)	Willy Boeckl (AUT)	Robert van Zeebroeck (BEL)
1932 Lake Placid, USA	Karl Schafer (AUT)	Gillis Crafstrom (SWE)	Montgomery Wilson (CAN)
1936 Garmisch, GER	Karl Schafer (AUT)	Ernst Baler (GER)	Felix Kaspar (AUT)
1940, 1944	**No Olympic Games Held**		
1948 St. Mortiz, SUI	Richard Button (USA)	Hans Gerschwiler (SUI)	Edi Rada (AUT)
1952 Oslo, NOR	Richard Button (USA)	Helmut Seibt (AUT)	James Grogan (USA)
1956 Cortina, ITA	Hayes Jenkins (USA)	Ronald Robertson (USA)	David Jenkins (USA)
1960 Squaw Valley, USA	David Jenkins (USA)	Karol Divin (CZE)	Donald Jackson (CAN)
1964 Innsbruck, AUT	Manfred Schnelldorfer (FRG)	Alain Calmat (FRA)	Scott Allen (USA)
1968 Grenoble, FRA	Wolfgang Schwarz (AUT)	Tim Wood (USA)	Patrick Pera (FRA)
1972 Sapporo, JPN	Ondrej Nepela (CZE)	Sergei Chetverukhin (URS)	Patrick Pera (FRA)
1976 Innsbruck, AUT	John Curry (GBR)	Vladimir Kovalev (URS)	Toller Cranston (CAN)
1980 Lake Placcid, USA	Robin Cousins (GBR)	Jan Hoffman (GDR)	Charles Tickner (USA)
1984 Sarajevo, YUG	Scott Hamilton (USA)	Brian Orser (CAN)	Jozef Sabovtchik (CZE)
1988 Calgary, CAN	Brian Baitano (USA)	Brian Orser (CAN)	Viktor Petrenko (URS)
1992 Albertville, FRA	Viktor Petrenko (EUN)	Paul Wylie (USA)	Peter Barna (CZE)

OLYMPIC WINTER GAMES

LADIES' SINGLES

	GOLD	SILVER	BRONZE
1908 London, GBR	Madge Syers (GBR)	Elsa Rendschmidt (GER)	Dorothy Greenhough (GBR)
1920 Antwerp, BEL	Magda Julin- Mauroy (SWE)	Svea Noren (SWE)	Theresa Weld (USA)
1924 Chamonix, FRA	Herma Plank- Szabo (AUT)	Beatrix Loughran (USA)	Ethel Muckelt (GBR)
1928 St. Moritz, SUI	Sonja Henie (NOR)	Fritzi Burger (AUT)	Beatrix Loughran (USA)
1932 Lake Placid, USA	Sonja Henie (NOR)	Fritzi Burger (AUT)	Maribel Vinson (USA)
1936 Garmisch, GER	Sonja Henie (NOR)	Cecilia Colledge (GBR)	Vivi-Anne Hulten (SWE)
1940, 1944	**No Olympic Games Held**		
1948 St. Moritz, SUI	Barbara Ann Scott (CAN)	Eva Pawlik (AUT)	Jeannette Altwegg (GBR)
1952 Oslo, NOR	Jeannette Altwegg (GBT)	Tenley Albright (USA)	Jacqueline de Bief (FRA)
1956 Cortina, ITA	Tenley Albright (USA)	Carol Heiss (USA)	Ingrid Wendl (AUT)
1960 Squaw Valley, USA	Carol Heiss (USA)	Sjoukje Dijkstra (HOL)	Barbara Roles (USA)
1964 Innsbruck, AUT	Sjoukje Dijkstra (HOL)	Regine Heitzer (AUT)	Petra Burka (CAN)
1968 Grenoble, FRA	Peggy Fleming (USA)	Gabriele Seyfert (GDR)	Hana Maskova (CZE)
1972 Sapporo, JPN	Beatrix Schuba (AUT)	Karen Magnussen (CAN)	Janet Lynn (USA)
1976 Innsbruck, AUT	Dorothy Hamill (USA)	Dianne de Leeuw (HOL)	Christine Errath (GDR)
1980 Lake Placid, USA	Anett Poetzsch (GDR)	Linda Fratianne (USA)	Dagmar Lurz (FRG)
1984 Sarajevo, YUG	Katarina Witt (GDR)	Rosalynn Sumners (USA)	Kira Ivanova (URS)
1988 Calgary, CAN	Katarina Will (GDR)	Elizabeth Manley (CAN)	Debi Thomas (USA)

	GOLD	SILVER	BRONZE
1992 Albertville, FRA	Kristi Yamaguchi (USA)	Midori Ito (JPN)	Nancy Kerrigan (USA)

OLYMPIC WINTER GAMES

PAIRS

	GOLD	SILVER	BRONZE
1908 London, GBR	Anna Hubler Heinrich Burger (GER)	Phyllis Johnson James Johnson (GBR)	Madge Syers Edgar Syers (GBR)
1920 Antwerp, BEL	Ludowika Jakobsson Walter Jakobsson (FIN)	Alexia Bryn Yngvar Byrn (NOR)	Phyllis Johnson Basil Williams (GBR)
1924 Chamonix, FRA	Helene Engelmann Alfred Berger (AUT)	Ludowika Jakobsson Walter Jakobsson (FIN)	Andree Brunet Pierre Brunet (FRA)
1928 St. Mortiz, SUI	Andree Brunet Pierre Burnet (FRA)	Lilly Scholz Otto Kaiser (AUT)	Melitta Brunner Ludwig Wrede (AUT)
1932 Lake Placid, USA	Andree Brunet Pierre Brunet (FRA)	Beatrix Loughran Sherwin Badger (USA)	Emilie Rotter Laszlo Szollas (HUN)
1936 Garmisch, GER	Maxie Herber Ernst Baier (GER)	Ilse Pausin Erich Pausin (AUT)	Emilie Rotter Laszlo Szollas (HUN)
1940, 1944	**No Olympic Games Held**		
1948 St. Moritz, SUI	Micheline Lannoy Pierre Baugnlet (BEL)	Andrea Kekesy Ede Kiraly (HUN)	Suzanne Morrow Wallace Distelmeyer (CAN)
1952 Oslo, NOR	Ria Falk Paul Falk (FRG)	Karol Kennedy Peter Kennedy (USA)	Marianne Nagy Laszlo Nagy (HUN)
1956 Cortina, ITA	Elizabeth Schwarz Kurt Oppelt (AUT)	Frances Dafoe Norris Bowden (CAN)	Marianne Nagy Laszlo Nagy (HUN)
1960 Squaw Valley, USA	Barbara Wagner Robert Paul (CAN)	Marika Kilius Hans Baumler (FRG)	Nancy Ludington Ronald Ludington (USA)

	GOLD	**SILVER**	**BRONZE**
1964 Innsbruck, AUT	Ludmila Belousova Oleg Protopopov (URS)	Marika Kilius Hans Baumler* (FRG)	Debbi Wilkes Guy Revell (CAN)

* Proven after the games that they had signed a show contract prior to the games. Silver went to Revell and Wilkes. Bronze went to Ronald and Vivian Joseph, USA.

1968 Grenoble, FRA	Ludmila Protopopov Oleg Protopopov (URS)	Tatiana Joukchesternava Alexandr Gorelik (URS)	Margot Glockshuber Wolfgang Danne (FRG)
1972 Sapporo, JPN	Irina Rodnina Alexel Ulanov (URS)	Ludmila Smirnova Andrei Suralkin (URS)	Manuela Gross Uwe Kagelmann (GDR)
1976 Innsbruck, AUT	Irina Rodnina Aleksandr Zaitsev (URS)	Romy Kermer Rolf Osterreich (GDR)	Manuela Gross Uwe Kagelmann (GDR)
1980 Lake Placid, USA	Irina Rodnina Aleksandr Zaitsev (URS)	Marina Cherkosova Sergei Shakrai (URS)	Manuella Mager Uwe Bewersdorff (GDR)
1984 Sarajevo, YUG	Elena Valova Oleg Vassilev (URS)	Caitlin Carruthers Peter Carruthers (USA)	Larissa Selezneva Oleg Makarov (URS)
1988 Calgary, CAN	Ekaterina Gordeeva Sergei Grinkov (URS)	Elena Valova Oleg Vasillev (URS)	Jill Watson Peter Oppegard (USA)
1992 Albertville, FRA	Natalia Mishkutenok Artur Dmitriev (EUN)	Elena Bechke Denis Petrov (EUN)	Isabelle Brasseur Lloyd Eisler (CAN)

OLYMPIC WINTER GAMES

ICE DANCING

	GOLD	**SILVER**	**BRONZE**
1976 Innsbruck, AUT	Ludmilla Pakhomova Alleksandr Gorshkov (URS)	Irina Moiseeva Andrei Minenkov (URS)	Colleen O'Connor Jim Millns (USA)

	GOLD	SILVER	BRONZE
1980 Lake Placid, USA	Gennadi Karponosov Natalia Lininchuk (URS)	Krisztina Regoczy Andras Sallay (HUN)	Irina Moiseeva Andrei Minenkov (URS)
1984 Sarajevo, YUG	Jayne Torvill Christopher Dean (GBR)	Natalia Bestemianova Andrei Bukin (URS)	Marina Klimova Sergei Ponomarenko (URS)
1988 Calgary, CAN	Natalia Bestemianova Andrei Bukin (URS)	Marina Klimova Sergei Ponomarenko (URS)	Tracy Wilson Robert McCall (CAN)
1992 Albertville, FRA	Marina Kilmova Sergei Ponomarenko (EUN)	Isabelle Duchesnay Paul Duchesnay (FRA)	Maia Usova Alexander Zhulin (EUN)

OLYMPIC WINTER GAMES
U.S. FINISHERS

MEN'S SINGLES

1908	Irving Brokaw (6)	
1920	Nathaniel Niles (6)	
1924	Nathaniel Niles (6)	
1928	Roger Turner (10) Nathaniel Niles (15)	Sherwin Badger (11)
1932	Roger Turner (6) Gail Borden (8)	James Madden (7) William Nagel (11)
1936	Robin Lee (12) George Hill (22)	Erie Reiter (13)
1948	Richard Button (1) James Grogan (6)	John Lettengarver (4)
1952	Richard Button (1) Hayes Alan Jenkins (4)	James Grogan (3)
1956	Hayes Alan Jenkins (1) David Jenkins (3)	Ronald Robertson (2)
1960	David Jenkins (1) Robert Brewer (7)	Tim Brown (5)
1964	Scott Allen (3) Monty Hoyt (10)	Thomas Litz (6)
1968	Timothy Wood (92) John Misha Petkevich (6)	Gary Viscontl (5)

1972	Kenneth Shelley (4)	John Misha Petkevich (5)
	Gordon McKellen (10)	
1976	David Santee (6)	Terry Kubicka (7)
1980	Charles Tickner (3)	David Santee (4)
	Scott Hamilton (5)	
1984	Scott Hamilton (1)	Brian Boitano (5)
	Mark Cockerall (13)	
1988	Brian Boitano (1)	Christopher Bowman (7)
	Paul Wylie (10)	
1992	Paul Wylie (2)	Christopher Bowman (4)
	Todd Eldredge (10)	

OLYMPIC WINTER GAMES
U.S. FINISHERS

LADIES' SINGLES

1920	Therea Weld (3)	
1924	Beatrix Loughran (2)	Theresa Weld-Blanchard (4)
1928	Beatrix Loughran (3)	Maribel Vinson (4)
	Theresa Weld-Blanchard (10)	
1932	Maribel Vinson (3)	Margaret Bennett (11)
	Suzanne Davis (12)	Louise Weigel (14)
1936	Maribel Vinson (5)	Audrey Peppe (12)
	Louise Weigel (21)	Estelle Weigel (22)
1948	Yvonne Sherman (6)	Gretchen Merill (8)
	Eileen Seigh (11)	
1952	Tenley Albright (2)	Sonya Klopfer (4)
	Virginia Baxter (5)	
1956	Tenley Albright (1)	Carol Heiss (2)
	Catherina Luise Machado (8)	
1960	Carol Heiss (1)	Barbara Ann Roles (3)
	Laurence Owen (6)	
1964	Peggy Fleming (6)	Christine Haigler (7)
	Albertine Noyes (8)	
1968	Peggy Fleming (1)	Albertine Noyes (4)
	Janet Lynn (9)	
1972	Janet Lynn (3)	Julie Lynn Holmes (4)
	Suna Murray (12)	
1976	Dorothy Hamill (1)	Wendy Burge (6)
1980	Linda Fratianne (2)	Lisa-Marie Allen (5)
	Sandy Lenz (9)	

1984	Rosalynn Sumners (2)	Tiffany Chin (4)
	Elaine Zayak (6)	
1988	Debi Thomas (3)	Jill Trenary (4)
	Caryn Kadavy (Withdrew)	
1992	Kristi Yamaguchi (1)	Nancy Kerrigan (3)
	Tonya Harding (4)	

OLYMPIC WINTER GAMES
U.S. FINISHERS

PAIRS

1920	Theresa Weld/Nathaniel Niles (4)
1924	Theresa Weld-Blanchard/Nathaniel Niles (6)
1928	Beatrix Loughran/Sherwin Badger (4)
	Theresa Weld-Blanchard/Nathaniel Niles (9)
1932	Beatrix Loughran/Sherwin Badger (2)
	Gertrude Meredith/Joseph Savage (7)
1936	Maribel Vinson/George Hill (5)
	Grace Madden/James Madden (11)
1948	Yvonne Sherman/Robert Swenning (4)
	Karol Kennedy/Peter Kennedy (6)
1952	Karol Kennedy/Peter Kennedy (2)
	Janet Gerhauser/John Nightingale (6)
1956	Carole Anne Ormaca/Robin Greiner (5)
	Lucille Mary Ash/Sully Kothmann (7)
1957	Nancy Ludington/Ronald Ludington (3)
	Maribel Owen/Dudley Richards (10)
	Ila Ray Hadley/Ray Hadley (11)
1964	Vivian Joseph/Ronald Joseph (4)
	Judianne Fotheringill/Jerry Fotheringill (7)
	Cynthia Kauffman/Ronald Kauffman (8)
1968	Cynthia Kauffman/Ronald Kauffman (6)
	Sandi Sweitzer/Roy Wagelein (7)
	Alicia Starbuck/Kenneth Shelley (13)
1972	JoJo Starbuck/Kenneth Shelley (4)
	Melissa Militano/Mark Militano (7)
	Barbara Brown/Douglas Berndt (12)
1976	Tai Babilonia/Randy Gardner (5)
	Alice Cook/William Fauver (12)
1980	Caitlin Carruthers/Peter Carruthers (5)
	Sheryl Franks/Michael Botticelli (7)

1984	Caitlin Carruthers/Peter Carruthers (2)
	Jill Watson/Burt Lancon (6)
	Lee Ann Miller/William Fauver (10)
1988	Jill Watson/Peter Oppegard (3)
	Gillian Wachsman/Todd Waggoner (5)
	Natalie Seybold/Wayne Seybold (10)
1992	Natasha Kuchiki/Todd Sand (6)
	Calla Urbanski/Rocky Marval (10)
	Jenni Meno/Scott Wendland (11)

OLYMPIC WINTER GAMES
U.S. FINISHERS

ICE DANCING

1976	Colleen O'Connor/Jim Millns (3)
	Judi Genovesi/Kent Weigle (15)
	Susan Kelley/Andrew Stroukoff (17)
1980	Judy Blumberg/Michael Seibert (7)
	Stacey Smith/John Summers (9)
1984	Judy Blumberg/Michael Seibert (4)
	Carol Fox/Richard Dalley (5)
	Elise Spitz/Scott Gregory (10)
1988	Suzanne Semanick/Scott Gregory (6)
	Susan Wynne/Joseph Druar (11)
1992	April Sargent-Thomas/Russ Witherby (11)
	Rachel Mayer/Peter Breen (15)

ABOUT THE AUTHORS

Wayne Coffey is an award-winning sportswriter for *The New York Daily News* and the author of an eight-book series of Olympic biographies. He has covered three Olympics for the *News*.

Filip Bondy, former Olympic reporter for *The New York Times*, is an award-winning columnist for *The New York Daily News* and among the most knowledgeable observers of the figure-skating world.

Wayne Coffey and Filip Bondy will be in Lillehammer, Norway covering the Winter Olympics for *The New York Daily News*.